THE CORPORATE SAMURAI

Ray Faulkenberry, PhD

iUniverse, Inc.
New York   Bloomington

THE CORPORATE SAMURAI
A New Model for Business Owners

iUniverse books may be ordered through booksellers or by contacting:

iUniverse
1663 Liberty Drive
Bloomington, IN 47403
www.iuniverse.com
1-800-Authors (1-800-288-4677)

ISBN: 978-0-595-46911-6 (pbk)
ISBN: 978-0-595-71061-4 (cloth)
ISBN: 978-0-595-91198-1 (ebk)

Printed in the United States of America

Testimonials

"This book is of great relevance at a time when technology is in many ways driving us to be more and more isolated from the rest of the world. Ray is stressing that the human and spiritual connection between us all is an essential element to corporate and daily personal living. Possibly the most important aspect of this book is reworking how we, as product and service providers, look at that which we provide to the public. In dropping the focus from the 'bottom line', and making sure that our product or service can benefit others - our organizations can only expect greater growth and benefit ... not to mention what it can do for this global economy that we live in. I recommend that every employer read this book and begin on your path towards enlightenment. Not only will your staff thank you, but your consumers will as well."

Lauren Skowronski – State Director of Organizing, Center for Civic Responsibility, New Jersey

----

I truly resonate with the honor and integrity in which this book was written. Ray comes from a place of deep compassion for his fellow man and it bleeds through on every page. It is clear that if every CEO takes this method of organizing and running their business, the very way business is done would change. Business's BOTTOM LINE would soar while every employee would feel a great sense of value and purpose!

Lincoln Ong, Ong Consulting LLC.

The Corporate Samurai stretches our current paradigm of the business world and emphasizes the importance of fusing both individual and corporate goals into ones professional life.

John Sweeney, Consultant, Accenture, National Security Division

----

Dr. Ray Faulkenberry has transformed a profound personal understanding of what truly makes humans happy and fulfilled into an enlightening new approach to cultivating a wealthy *and* healthy corporate environment. As Dr. Faulkenberry points out, the very qualities that people crave in their everyday lives -- compassion, honesty, integrity, love and vision -- are also vitally important in the workplace. By adopting the simple methods of the Corporate Samurai, any manager can easily maximize employee satisfaction and profits all at once! The Corporate Samurai is a wonderful book for anyone in a management position who cares about their employees' quality of life. Whether it be managing an office of two, or a corporation of 20,000, Dr. Faulkenberry offers a compelling case for applying the methods of the Corporate Samurai to any business environment to acheive unprecedented levels of success. Dr. Faulkenberry's book is easy to read, easy to understand and -- best of all -- easy to apply.

Alexander S. Gese, Attorney at Law Robins, Kaplan, Miller & Ciresi, LLP

"This simple little book can take business philosophy and leadership to a new level. Honoring and appreciating all those involved in the business process, as Ray Faulkenberry knows and teaches us, is what it is all about."

-Mike Robbins, author of *Focus on the Good Stuff*

"An ancient world inspires a new vision brought to us by a new visionary. The nobility of our business leaders is more powerful than their swords. Here is a vision of what true success can be."

Rev. David McArthur , CEO of Unity Center, Walnut Creek, California

---

A very interesting concept on how a CEO should run a business. Going beyond just caring about the bottom line of a company, to actually caring about the employees and their family. Looking at your employees as if they are separate important entities and not just a number. Finding out what their goals, ambitions, beliefs and financial needs are in order to make them more productive and genuinely happier at their jobs and with their personal lives.

Will corporate America (or even just bosses, managers or foremen) adapt to this kind of structure? We can only hope so.

Bob Teal
Manager/Associate
Structural Engineering Firm

To my mother and father, Morris and Pat Faulkenberry. Although my mother is no longer with us, both she and my father always entertained an entrepreneurial spirit. They enthusiastically embraced so many dreams and pushed to find the one that would bring them to the promised land. Although they never found that elusive pot at the end of the rainbow, the never-ending journey they embarked on has always inspired me.

Thank you, Mom and Dad, for all that you have done for me.

Contents

ACKNOWLEDGEMENTS

Every book begins as a thought, an itch, something that persists and doesn't go away. *The Corporate Samurai* began the first time I witnessed a business transaction. It was in those early memories that the seed for me to go into business may have been planted. I say *may* because I still stand in awe and wonderment of all the pearls of wisdom that arrive through means we may not be aware of.

I have been blessed to have special people in my life who have helped shape me and helped me to realize what truly is important in my life.

No acknowledgment could even begin without mentioning my wife, Linda. I can still remember laying eyes on you for the first time and felt something true in the vision of loveliness that came in the door that day. The evolutionary journey we've taken since that day in 1980 has been truly wondrous. Although we have had our ups and downs, this walk together in life has been the most incredible relationship a man could ever hope for. You've made a wonderful companion to me, and I feel blessed every day that you've had enough wisdom for the both of us when, at various times in our relationship, I couldn't decipher right from wrong, healthy from unhealthy.

Thank you, Linda, for being there through all of it.

Next comes my son, Wes.

Since you were born in November of 1993, you've grown into an amazing young man and someone I have come to value deeply in my life. I never thought I would have a son and feel this way about him. Your unconditional love for me is revealed every day of my life and is the most amazing thing I have ever experienced. Even when I don't deserve it, you are on my side and there to protect me. I feel your love so strongly that it almost leaves me breathless. My son wants to go into the family business with me, to provide opportunities for others, serve the planet, and take his place as a conscious steward of the earth. I can't wait for him to join my business team so we can spend the rest of our lives working to help others in whatever ways we can.

Sixteen months after Wes was born, his little sister Meaghan slid into the world almost four months early and weighing only a pound and a half. Although most didn't think she'd make it, she proved them wrong and has been an incredible asset to our family and my life. Meaghan, the depth and compassion that you showed from an early age told me you were an old soul. I have always felt that you would have as much to teach your mother and me as we would ever have to teach you. Since your birth in 1995, my prophecy has proved accurate. Thank you for blessing our lives. You are a daily inspiration, and I will always see you as my little angel.

Since this book is truly about relationships, I must acknowledge those relationships that have helped me grow in my mind and heart. My nuclear family—consisting of my mother and father, sisters Debbie and Vivian, along with my brother, Mike—have given me every blessing that any self-respecting adventurer in life could hope for. Even now, as we approach a half-century of being in the same family, I still draw wisdom, inspiration, and support from all of you. I know it's been a long, long journey. There are a lot of miles under the bridge, and many of those miles have been hard. I am grateful, humbled, and honored to have had you all in my life.

Also, to those who have moved through my life in the form of friends, colleagues, classmates, and co-workers, I say thank you. The lessons and support you gave me were vital in my learning and becoming the person I am now. I'm sorry if I ever took you for granted. As I look back, I couldn't have asked for a richer group of people to help me shape my life than all of you.

The last acknowledgment may seem kind of strange.

I truly wish to thank the quantum universe, which I could also call Spirit, God, and so many other names. I firmly believe we play a vital role in designing and creating our lives and that the incredible consciousness that created this universe is always present, always loving, and always helping us to create that which we most deeply wish to learn and experience. I am truly awed and deeply humbled at the incredible adventure that is this magnificent gift called life. Thank you, Divine Spirit, for your part in allowing me to play in this incredible game.

INTRODUCTION

You are a Samurai.

You may not think this is true but nevertheless the fact remains – you are Samurai. While you may think this book was strictly written for CEOs and business owners, it was not. You see, every one of us is the CEO of our life. It is we who are in control, make the decisions, plan the goals and strategies, and pull the trigger. While you may or may not be the actual CEO of your company, you weigh and make the decisions in your life and by nature are inherently Samurai.

As your read, you may get the sense that I am talking to Executive management or "the boss." I am and I'm not. I am talking to every person who works and makes decisions in their own life. If you are a CEO or business owner, consider what I say as it relates to shaping your company and your life. If you are not a CEO or business owner, consider what I say as it relates to shaping your life.

As Samurai, it is up to you to take charge of your life – both personally and professionally.

When most people think of the term *Samurai*, they think of a Japanese master swordsman—a fierce and disciplined warrior ready to kill when the need arises. While in some

1

Those around the Samurai honored their authority to rule, and although the Samurai could take anything they wanted by force, they most often used their minds and hearts to guide them, to the benefit of all.

cases this may have been true, the true Samurai was much more than a combat warrior. Thank God Tom Cruise made a movie a few years ago entitled *The Last Samurai.* The film introduced a lot of people to the depth and conscious actions by which the Samurai lived. Although Hollywood tends to overly dramatize many of its films, *The Last Samurai* beautifully depicts the heart and soul of what the Samurai believed.

In the film, Tom Cruise plays Nathan Algren, a Civil War hero who has found little meaning in his life after the war. He is paid by the Japanese government to train troops and hunt down the last Samurai. Algren is captured by the Samurai because his troops were forced into battle before they were ready.

Algren is forced to spend the harsh winter in the mountain village protected by the Samurai. He discovers the depth, beauty, wisdom, and love the Samurai has for his family, friends, and the emperor. His integrity is beyond reproach; he only wishes to serve the emperor and his country to the best of his ability. His ability to fight is only rivaled by his ability to witness beauty in all its shapes and forms. Algren sees the value in this and forms a unique friendship with the Samurai that lasts until their dying breaths.

This is not an advertisement for the film, although I found it excellent, but an effort to illustrate the qualities that the Samurai represented. Historically, those around the Samurai honored their authority to rule, and although the Samurai could take anything they wanted by force, they most often used their minds and hearts to guide them, to the benefit of all.

Wouldn't you say that this sentence might characterize an enlightened *CEO*?

3

It is time to take corporate CEOs and business owners to another level of functionality. They will have to be willing to look deep into their hearts and see what has meaning, not only for themselves, but for others as well. It's a journey rooted in empathy, compassion, love, empowerment, and stewardship.

As someone who has studied psychology at the doctoral level and counseled various individuals in various settings—ranging from alcohol and drug counseling to hypnotherapy to spiritual counseling—in addition to running my own businesses, I have watched and listened to and read a tremendous amount about current business and leadership practices, but I would not say that the above sentence accurately describes most business CEOs. It has been my observation that most business CEOs are first and foremost concerned about what is commonly known as the bottom line. How much money is the company making? Are our shares up? What does our current P & L look like? Are we growing, or is our business or field going through a recession?

When I was growing up, my father made his living hanging Sheetrock. Initially, he worked for others and then later on went into business for himself, forming a partnership with one of his best friends. I grew up thinking that people went to work to earn a living and pay their bills—nothing more, nothing less. When they got to work, they worked. When the whistle blew, they went home. They took their ten-minute break around 10:00 a.m., took their lunch for a half hour at noon, and then had another ten-minute break at 2:00 p.m. They put down their hammer and nails at 4:30 p.m.

When I was about eight years old, I spent my first summer working with my dad, brother, and my dad's partner and his son. I thought it was interesting that we always got to work about fifteen minutes before 8:00 a.m. My dad would sharpen his tools, pull the tabs off the Sheetrock, and grab a last cup of coffee. When the clock hit eight, he wasn't getting ready to work; he was putting the Sheetrock up on the wall—an honest day's work for an honest day's pay. As I have grown up and worked in various fields, I have seen fewer and fewer instances of this ethical trait. Oftentimes, people show up to work late, take extended breaks and lunches, and generally find ways to minimize

The Corporate Samurai is the enlightened CEO for the new age.

their work time. Obviously, this statement doesn't apply across the board; rather, it reflects a trend I've seen in many companies. It seems in today's business environments that the workers are oftentimes less committed than my father was.

Could this be because the employees are not happy in their jobs? Could it be that they don't feel valued by their employer? Are they not taken care of by their organization?

Before my father went into business with his partner a few years later, I never saw his employer do anything special for my father or his partner. There weren't any bonuses or raises or profit sharing. My father was a journeyman Sheetrocker, and when he had been in the field long enough, he topped out at his maximum hourly wage and stayed there. I guess, at that time, people may have been happy just to have a job. I know my father did not like his job, but he continued to install Sheetrock for years, even though it tore his body up. He eventually went into the "taping" phase of construction, and although this was less stressful on his body, it was still very physically demanding work.

I don't ever remember my father's boss providing any personal incentives or goals that would allow my father to achieve my father's goals. I don't believe my father's boss ever even asked what those goals might be. I know my father would have loved to be asked about his financial, social, and job goals. I believe his big bonus was getting a ham or a turkey around the holidays. While it made a nice little gift, it did nothing to enhance my father's career or life goals.

Even the job with which I've been most associated in the last ten years—an educational specialist—has neither done anything to enhance what I do as an individual nor helped me achieve my goals. As an educational specialist for a charter school here in the San Francisco Bay Area, working with "at-risk" young men and women between the ages of eighteen and twenty-five, I evaluate, plan, coordinate, and implement education plans for my students. In short, I am the evaluator, administrator, counselor, and teacher for my students, who are pursuing their high school diploma while working in the California Conservation Corps. I have received lots of training in order to achieve the company's goals, but the company has never even inquired what *my* goals are.

Again, I believe this to be the norm.

Most people in corporate positions spend vast amounts of money helping their employees learn ways to make them more productive *for the company.* January 2007 statistics released by *Entrepreneur Magazine* and Gallup indicate that almost 80% of people in the work force are unhappy in their current job. Over three hundred billion dollars are lost every year through poor job fit, employee dissatisfaction, and missed days (*Entrepreneur Magazine*, January 18, 2007). Employees often see an "us versus them" mentality, and the commitment to the company changes over the years, both from an employee's and employer's perspective. Employees don't want to put out the "extra" effort and begin doing only what their jobs require them to do. Employers also begin seeing employees as an expendable commodity, something easily replaced. Rare is the person who works his or her whole career for one company.

With the business cycle and the additional pressure to achieve a healthy bottom line, companies are forced to cut costs, and sometimes employees, to show the shareholder a yearly profit. What tends to happen is that more work is piled onto the remaining employees. Overwork, lack of recognition, stress, and burnout often result, which lead to a rapid turnover in the work force. Employers often see a never-ending supply of potential replacements for their workers and do not hesitate to share this information with the employee. Employees feel threatened and begin to stress and *push* in a way that throws not only their job but also their life out of balance. They take this stress into their family life, which can cause struggle that is not easily resolved.

If companies are to thrive, this process needs to change.

Some corporate CEOs and business owners are beginning to look at the benefits of creating a healthier work atmosphere. This has taken the shape of profit sharing, increased benefits, bonuses, discounts, or even paid memberships in health clubs. The term *job enrichment* has been used over the last couple of decades to encourage the better use of the employees' talents and skills. Some companies even provide structured leisure activities for employees, periodic activities geared toward recreation and leisure. Companies that are creating these new environments for their employees are definitely on the right track.

Even though some companies are making wonderful employee advancements, I believe the relationship between employer and employee can move to an even more productive level.

Our occupation, to a large extent, represents a balance of who we are, what we value, and what we want to contribute in the world. While there are many ways to contribute to society, our careers provide an opportunity to express who we are in specific ways. If we are only seen as a programmer, a clerk, a receptionist, or a manager, then we will contribute within the confines of our job description. If we are seen as an *unlimited resource* capable of planning and creating new elements and expanding our jobs even further, then we are potentially a key part of the company's success. Not only do people want to be recognized as cre-

Corporate Samurai live their lives with honor, integrity, authenticity, and a supreme desire to protect and empower those they have been privileged to lead.

ative and talented resources, they also want to contribute in a way that is meaningful and appreciated.

This book is not for people whose only concern in running their business or their corporation is the bottom line. Such people would be much better off learning how to operate with a sweatshop mentality, which some people think is good business practice, in order to enhance the company's profitability, raise shares, satisfy stockholders, and put more money in their own pockets. I am not interested in utilizing people solely for the benefit of my shareholders or myself. Nor am I interested in limiting people to doing mundane tasks. There is another way.

This book will focus on creating sustainable businesses and corporations that have an increased bottom line. I believe the greatest gift a business can give is tapping into the unlimited potential of its employees, to help them develop in all ways while the company makes a profit. In this way, employers will gain a higher purpose, both for themselves and for their business.

Enlightened CEOs will look to develop and enrich their employees' lives in every way. It is time that a new model is brought forth; it will help change our traditional, archaic methods of running businesses and corporations.

Don't get me wrong. I am not saying that a profitable business is not important—it truly is. I believe that profitable businesses run by good people create opportunities not only within the companies, but in communities as well. These enlightened businesses help to enlighten the community, which is the first step in causing the world to shift. Increased prosperity with the right mentality can and will change the world.

The end result will be an organization that works like a close family. While individuality is honored and respected, the environment of the business culture is geared to empowerment on every level—not just financial. It doesn't take a rocket scientist to know that if you have an organization that is authentically invested in each employee, you have the potential to create something special.

Not only will your business be sustainable and profitable, you will enhance the meaning of people's lives. One of my teacher colleagues was telling me the other day that counting the time getting ready for work, driving to work, working, and then driving home, the average person spends *half* his or her life involved with work. I don't know where my colleague heard that, but as I stop and think, it resonates as true. That is an amazing amount of time to devote to anything, much less a job that may not be fulfilling a person's hopes and dreams. By creating a relationship and business structure that recognizes the value of connecting with another human being, you will create a company that will truly amaze you.

People long to be connected in all phases of their lives. They want to belong to something they believe in. If we as business owners are willing to honor our employees to the deepest levels, they will explode with creativity, consciousness, appreciation, and improved job performance. We as business owners will prosper not only from the increased quality of work, but in truly engaging people deeply in their own lives. To be able to guide people to reach their most cherished goals strikes me as one of the most amazing gifts we could ever be a part of.

I am asking you, business owners and CEOs, to have the courage to look deeply into your business structure and entertain the thoughts and ideas within the book. In the wisdom of your own heart, I believe you will see that the points made and suggestions offered will resonate deeply within you. It will be up to you to have the courage to begin the integration.

As a martial arts instructor with a sixth-degree black belt in Tae Kwon Do and Kenpo, I often tell my students to draw their sword and face the dragon. I urge you to do the same. Draw your sword and face the dragon that holds you captive in your growth as a human being and as part of a corporate entity.

Draw your sword and face the dragon that holds you captive in your growth as a human and as part of a corporate entity.

Chapter One: What Truly Is Your Business?

In the introduction, I stated that the greatest gift a business can give is tapping into the unlimited potential of those people who have chosen to work for the company and develop them in *all ways*, while making a profit. We'd all like to work for or own a company like this, wouldn't we?

What truly is a business, then?

What do corporations do?

The University of Georgetown business department uses a definition of business that most people would agree with: "An enterprise, commercial entity, or firm in either the private or public sector, concerned with providing products or services to satisfy customer requirements."[1]

This makes sense, doesn't it?

Business owners and CEOs would tell you they are in business to provide goods or services, or both. They wish to supply a product or a service that the public or private sector can use. I agree with these statements.

I would then pose the following question and ask you to stop and think deeply about the reasons you might give as an answer.

Why are you providing the goods and/or services that you do?

Recently, I got on the phone and asked this question of fifty-seven CEOs of various types and sizes of businesses. Although I did not adhere to any rigorous protocol, five answers were consistently mentioned.

1. Money

"If I or my company creates this product or service, we can sell it to the world and make money. The more we sell, the more money we make. The more money our company makes, the more money I make. The more money I make, the more things I can buy and do."

This was the gist of the most common statement CEOs made regarding money.

This is a logical theory for why we go into business and, to a large extent, fits for many or most of us. All of us would like to have more money. If we made enough money, we could buy a nice car, wear nice clothes, live in a nice house, go on nice vacations, and more.

Experiencing prosperity in our own lives due to the success of our business would be wonderful. To see the fruits of our labors paying off and finally hitting "Easy Street" would evoke a feeling that most people in the world would love to experience. What I want you as the new CEO to develop is the feeling of sharing the wealth by taking part of your and the company's prosperity and not only sharing with employees but also reaching outward into the community to spread wealth.

It's not hard to set up a profit-sharing plan, even in small companies. In the church I attend, where I serve on the board, we're not always in the black. Despite this fact, we always give 10% of our income to various charitable organizations. We also give all employees a bonus to let them know how much we appreciate them and the honor of working alongside them. As I move forward in the companies that I'm launching, (We R One Productions, Conscious Media, Inc., and the Institute for World Transformation), I will also take 10% of the profit for the year and disburse it among the employees. As our company grows and profits increase, so will the amount we are able to give as employee bonuses. Even when the amount is not large, the employee appreciates being thought of and knowing that management cares.

The Samurai model mandates we begin to expand our reach— our influence to help those around us in an ever-widening circle. Once you've taken care of your employees financially, you can look outward into the community. If you're a smaller business, get involved at a local level. There are many wonderful nonprofit organizations and schools in every community that would greatly benefit from any financial gift. If you're not sure which to choose, contact me. Our nonprofit, the Institute for World Transformation, would love to receive your gift!

What is something that you and your company feel passionate about? There are many ways to act on something your company is passionate about.

Truly one of the great pleasures of the world is deciding what cause your company wants to support. The gift of giving doesn't have to be limited to finances. Many organizations need volunteers to provide services and general support. Mentoring people is another gift we can give other companies and organizations. The only limit to a company's giving is the limit of any lack of creativity.

As your company grows, in addition to your local giving, you can reach out into your state or region and support larger programs. Some organizations have become national sponsors and give to many organizations. These corporations often move beyond our country's borders and reach out to those in need in other parts of the world.

A universal principle states that the universe abhors a vacuum, and when you give of yourself, you create a vacuum that the universe immediately begins to fill, all because of your willingness to share.

It was said that John D. Rockefeller gave away millions of dollars over the course of his lifetime to people on the street because he knew that the gift and the reward was in the giving. He also knew, based on the vacuum principle, that one of the best ways for him to increase his fortune was to give it away. This principle states that the universe abhors a vacuum and that you whatever you give out, more will be returned to you.

I heard recently that Warren Buffett, the world's second-richest man, is going to give over 85% of his wealth to the Bill and Melinda Gates Foundation.[2] At present, Buffett's fortune is estimated at well over $40 billion! The Gates foundation's activities, internationally famous, are focused on world health—fighting such diseases as malaria, HIV/AIDS, and tuberculosis—and on improving U.S. libraries and high schools. What an amazing gift! Warren Buffett will always be rich, as the universe will continue to replenish what Mr. Buffett so freely gives.

2. Expansion

Expansion without consciousness is like a virus. It spreads, creates havoc, and destroys.

A lot of companies provide the goods and services that they do because they truly believe that the public and/or private sector greatly benefits from those goods or services. When it becomes successful, they may wish to expand their business and open up other centers or expand their product lines.

I like the idea of expansion; if you truly feel you are providing a valuable product or service to your community, why not expand and offer it to more people? I truly believe that is a wonderful by-product of doing good business. If you're doing something right that benefits people, why not do it on a larger scale?

Expanding and growing is healthy, whether it's in our personal or professional lives. The main question is to ask *why* we are choosing to expand.

> *Do we want to expand?*
> *Do we need to expand?*
> *What will we, as a company, gain by expanding?*
> *What will I, as an individual, gain by expanding?*
> *What will my employees gain from the expansion?*
> *What will my community gain by our expanding?*
> *How will this expansion serve the vision of improving the planet?*

A lot of people may think these questions are inconsequential. However, if you and your company are trying to exist in a more aware or enlightened state, these questions may warrant serious attention. To expand without a defined reason or purpose is like sailing a ship out into the ocean without a destination or a compass.

I know a man who has an organization that bids on the contracts to run Job Corps centers around the country. At present, there are approximately 126 of these federally funded programs. Job Corps provides food, housing, education, and training for young men and women between the ages of sixteen and twenty-four. It is a wonderful organization that strives to educate and guide young people into the next phase of their lives.

This gentleman holds the contracts to approximately one dozen of these centers. He makes a wonderful living and recently shared that he had to rent a warehouse in order to store all of his cars. Although his company is very successful, he is the kind of person who has demonstrated the ability to steal from others.

Some dear friends of mine proposed a program that would do incredible things for their Job Corps students and would provide a detailed transition plan once they left the Job Corps program. This program was more than anything anyone had ever seen or imagined and would help the students in ways that would not benefit only them, but also the Job Corps Center and the organization as a whole. Instead of honoring my friends who proposed this program, the owner of the company stated to his board that since the people came to him without copyrights for the program, he saw no reason to employ them. He proposed that Job Corps just take the concept and develop it itself. Fortunately, two of his high-ranking employees recognized this as unethical and stated that they wanted nothing to do with the proposal unless my friends were involved. Perturbed, the owner of the company became angry and upset at these individuals, but because they provided great value to his company, he did not fire them. He shelved the project and blew off the program.

This, to me, illustrates the arrogance and greed that often envelop those in powerful positions. CEOs and executives who run unethical companies are focused on personal recognition, money, and power. The gentleman mentioned above did not think about honoring those kind enough to bring their idea to him, nor did he honor his mandate to provide the best service possible to his Job Corps students.

It saddened me to hear this story; I could sense that this CEO's choices discounted many valuable people. Instead of creating a win/win/win situation, he was looking for the best way for himself and his company to win. In essence, he sought ways to look better and put even more money in his pocket. He had a wonderful opportunity to not only provide a valuable new service to his kids, but also to grow as an organization—not to mention to allow my friends to grow in their pursuit of aiding and developing their programs.

This type of choice creates a stagnant environment in which the same old people keep doing the same old things. It is not a state of evolution or growth, and such a mentality contributes to employee burnout, job dissatisfaction, high turnover, and general poor performance throughout the organization. Samurai ethics teach us to be in the moment, look at what is immediately in front of us, and strive to see the beauty and perfection in the moment. I know that sounds philosophical, but it is strictly a matter of perspective.

Expansion started from within is the best method for any individual aspiring to reach Samurai status. It's important to ponder and meditate on expanding one's vision about how to create a healthier, more efficient company. The Samurai looks only to grow and expand by being consciously aware of what is around him at all times. From this place of awareness, he can determine what needs to be done, communicate it in an efficient manner, and show compassion and appreciation for those involved and engaged in the process.

3. Power and Freedom

Power is another key concept in developing one's company and one's life. Power, if used wisely, can allow people to feel confident enough to explore and expand their current style of being and doing. Those who allow their hearts to guide their power can support and nurture the people they guide and supervise. People who use their power with the benefit of others in mind are much more open to the creative process that allows new discoveries and ideas to come forth and further develop the company. Power properly used magnetizes other people to the individuals in power in a positive way.

This last paragraph says a lot of wonderful things about power when it's properly utilized. If we are empowering in our organization, we instill confidence in our employees and encourage them to stretch, grow, and take risks that are positive and expansive in nature. Individuals who feel empowered by their employers are much more likely to be creative and to look for

The Samurai model mandates we begin to expand our reach—our influence to help those around us in an ever-widening circle.

Expansion without consciousness is like a virus. It spreads, creates havoc, and destroys.

To expand without a defined reason or purpose is like sailing a ship out into the ocean without a destination or a compass.

ways to enhance the company, their products, and their customers. They feel secure in knowing they can bring their entire creative force to the table to enhance not only their jobs, but the company's vision and goals as well.

If you, the CEO/supervisor, constantly encourage from a sincere place in your heart, you will allow your employees to feel supported and freer to push their limits in achieving their assignments. Then it doesn't feel like a job, but an opportunity to use the gifts and resources they brought into this world and further developed throughout their lives.

Not only does this sincere empowerment lift your employees up, it makes them feel supported. If you've also given them a fair compensation package, then you're starting on the right path to creating a truly meaningful work experience for your employees that will yield long-term benefits for you both.

However, if you are among the multitude of CEOs and business owners who don't fully support the development of your employee's creativity, emotional health, or financial goals, then you not only have a disgruntled employee, but someone whose best work is still trapped inside. These people will come to their *job* and go to *work*.

Sound like fun?

It is my opinion that true power is not conveyed by the title of the individual. The true proof of power is in one's ability to instill hope, enthusiasm, passion, and satisfaction in others. It's an ongoing process of nurturing, honoring, and supporting. Anything less and you might as well wield the taskmaster's whip.

The true Samurai did not have to push his power on others. He did not have to brag, boast, or belittle others. The Samurai's power came from knowing who he was, what his life represented, and how he wanted to be in each and every moment.

He led his people with the strength that came from the union of his heart and mind, not his sword.

4. Fame (The Legacy)

Fame is a fascinating concept. I've always felt that the attraction to fame is, in its higher sense, our desire to be remembered, to know that we've lived a life of meaning. That we have to be recognized and be "famous" may stem from us not feeling significant, deep within ourselves. However, feeling unique or appreciated is something that we all value and, in some ways, it comes from the same energy as the desire for fame. Toward the end of the book we'll be talking about the importance of building our legacy in order to organize and live the life we desire and to feel connected to the goals we wish to accomplish.

When I was in my early twenties, I worked for a residential treatment center for emotionally disturbed boys in the Sierra foothills. The executive director at the time used to take me with him on occasion to visit candidates for our program in various county juvenile halls. He would tell the kids the following, with which I did not agree either then or now: "You are going to be judged in society by what you do and how well you do it."

I believe, for a lot of people, the above sentence is true. I know we are evaluated to a certain extent based on our skills and proficiency. I personally prefer to see people from a perception that I choose to see them from and not judge them by how well they work on cars, write computer programs, or try cases. What I mean is that I have a choice in every moment about how I perceive anyone or anything. I can choose to see them with the depth of my heart, or I can see them impersonally, as expendable assets to use as I see fit—or anywhere in between. In my opinion, this executive director was pushing the young men toward the belief that we are only as good as our skills, and if we don't have skills, we will be judged harshly.

I don't wish to get into a long debate about the ethics of this statement; I can see merit on both sides. I feel, however, that if we're pushing to develop great skills so we can be evaluated by society in a positive way, then we are searching for external validation based on what we do versus *who we are*. Fame provides external validation. The world recognizes us, therefore we feel more valued. It's a fine line between being and feeling appreciated and seeking and coveting fame.

Feeling unique and appreciated and wanting to build a legacy worthy and representative of the life we live is, to me, a much healthier choice than seeking power and fame. Creating a legacy that others can grow with and build on is embracing a model of stewardship that will greatly benefit the evolution of our planet.

The Samurai was not concerned with fame. The mission was to be true to himself; living a life of integrity and honor was the most important thing. If fame came to the Samurai, it was not because he coveted it. The Samurai would say that one who covets fame cannot be focused on the moment and will miss the next great moment of life because of his preoccupation with fame. The Samurai's words and actions spoke volumes, and the fame that accompanied his actions was carried by others. Fame was something for others to comment on, not the Samurai. A Samurai's legacy was kept alive by those who witnessed his actions and then chose to share them with their children and those in the community.

5. Product or Service

The best reason I can think of for going into business is to provide a necessary service for our community or society. By determining what is needed and could enhance our quality of life, we are looking to grow beyond what we currently have or experience. This is evolution. It is a mindset that I feel is spiritually enlightening. If we can be conscious of providing a product or service for the benefit for those around us and trust

Samurai ethics teach us to be in the moment, look at what is immediately in front of us, and strive to see the beauty and perfection in the moment.

Remember: the true test of power comes from one's ability to instill hope, enthusiasm, passion, and satisfaction in others.

that the act of providing this product or service is the true victory, then we have discovered the inherent joy of business.

Notice the difference between this concept and what I've been describing up to this point.

What we've been talking about before revolved around getting what *we want*. Through awareness of what could improve the quality of our lives or make our lives more comfortable or efficient, and making that a catalyst for business, we are looking out for the *benefit of others*. What I mean by this is that if you as a CEO can be more aware of the qualities you value in yourself, you can be more empathetic and compassionate in seeing those qualities in your employees. You can come up with rational and meritorious reasons for going into business, but it is my heartfelt opinion that unless you go into business with the concept of serving and making the world a better place, you're in self-absorbed mode.

That's not enlightened business and is not the way of the Samurai.

The Samurai did what was necessary, when it was necessary, for the good of all. To him, it was an honor to provide a service for the benefit of others. Everything the Samurai did was geared toward making the lives of people he protected richer, happier, and more fulfilling. The service he provided was embodying justice, compassion, and leadership.

Isn't that a nice description of our concept of the Corporate Samurai?

Isn't that also a nice description of an evolved human being?

Wouldn't it be great if people went to work knowing that their CEO, director, or supervisor was looking after them in that way?

The Samurai was not concerned with fame. The mission was to be true to himself; living a life of integrity and honor was the most important thing.

How committed would employees be to a company that honored them in this way?

Wouldn't it feel wonderful to be a CEO, director, or supervisor and know you were taking care of your employees like that?

Virtually every spiritual tradition advocates giving rather than receiving. It is also a common spiritual thought that as we give, so shall we receive. We grow up hearing from good souls all the time about the merit and joy of giving.

How do we efficiently give to our business, employees, community, and the world?

When approached from the right perspective, any business can come from the heart with the goal of *serving*.

Let me share with you some insights I gained in learning to become a modern-day Samurai.

When I was young and first exposed to the martial arts, I was totally fascinated. Bruce Lee flying around on the movie screen with lightning-fast kicks and punches went beyond my comprehension of how the body could move. Even though Bruce was a small man—five foot seven and only 130 pounds—the power and intimidation he created on the screen and in real life were amazing. After Bruce's movies left the theaters in 1973, there wasn't much martial art to watch, as there were no videos, DVD's, or modern cable system. Occasionally, on a late Saturday night, I could catch on an obscure channel some old, badly dubbed martial arts film. Such films usually showcased the same actors, and they choreographed their moves into preset routines that were, for the most part, totally unrealistic. Films have come a long way since then with their stage combat and special effects. Movies like *The Matrix* and *Crouching Tiger, Hidden Dragon* have taken cinematic fighting to a previously unimagined level.

*The Samurai did what was
necessary, when it was necessary,
for the good of all. To him, it was
an honor to provide a service
for the benefit of others.*

When I was thirteen and saw Bruce's classic film *Enter the Dragon* with my grandmother at our local drive-in, I couldn't help but notice that Bruce lived and studied in a monastery. Their monastery was about living together in harmony—studying and learning about life and each other. Bruce, while being a great fighter within the temple, still tutored young students in *being*.

Television's series *Kung Fu* brought me another step closer to this concept. David Carradine's characterization of a Shaolin monk took me further into the depth of martial arts. His character, Kwai Chang Caine, was a hunted priest who roamed the Old West after fleeing China for avenging the death of his master at the hand of the emperor's nephew.

At this time of my life, the physical fighting on the screen wasn't what held my attention—it was the philosophy and manner in which this man lived his life. He came from a place of simple joy and appreciation. He looked not to harm a soul but to honor life and bring peace wherever he went. He was not overly concerned for his own material possessions, as he found joy in living and connecting with life around him.

When I decided to open up my own martial arts school in my mid-twenties, I had to make a decision. The martial arts system I had learned and studied came from a strict "combat mentality." We focused 99% of our time on what I call the "punch, kick, smash" method of martial arts. While we got in good shape and learned how to pummel someone, very little of the training moved anywhere near the heart and spirit I wanted to pursue.

I had started my doctorate in psychology and was gaining more and more insights into spiritual principles of love, kindness, compassion, and service, and my view of what to teach in my martial arts school became blurred. Although I continued to teach the traditional combat style I had learned, I began learning other styles that were less focused on offense and began sharing them with my students. I also began an Awareness

The goal of the Corporate Samurai is to provide the resources that allow their employees to live richer, fuller lives.

Class that met once a week for a few hours, in which the students and I got together and talked. We discussed the beauty and depth of life and marital arts and how to better apply this in our daily lives.

The Awareness Class and the school became more popular. We quickly outgrew our location and had to rent twice the space to keep up with the influx of students. I found that people wanted this depth; they wanted to grow, stretch, and move in a direction that I believe deeply resonates within our spirits. It is a direction of authenticity, honor, integrity, love, compassion, and service. I knew my inner Samurai was emerging through reaching out from the depth of my being to others who were also looking to discover their own inner depth. I did all I could at that time to provide opportunities for my students to grow.

This experience, more than any in my life, brought me into the powerful realization that providing a service that people could use in a way that carried deep meaning for them was the greatest gift I could offer the planet and a worthy direction for my life's path. It allowed me to give from my heart and deeply honor those people who were kind enough to want to come and train with me. I can think of no higher honor than to have individuals look to you for insight into becoming healthier, happier, and more productive human beings who are fully present in their time on earth. This is not unlike the ancient Samurai who would give their life to be of service to the emperor.

It was at this time in my life that I realized I was on the path to becoming a modern-day Samurai.

When you believe that people want this depth, wherever they are in their career path or in life, then you can reach out to them with your heart in a way that goes so much deeper than the superficiality of drawing a paycheck and helping you increase your bottom line. You would be committing yourself to making a difference—possibly first and foremost in your own life. However, stop in this moment and imagine yourself in either position—the CEO or the employee—and feel the energy that you would experience by taking this new approach to business.

It doesn't feel good. It feels *incredible.*
You can say, "Well, I'm not running a martial arts school."

I understand this. You're providing a product or a service.

Yet the ability to lead from the heart transcends martial arts. It speaks directly to the essence of being a Samurai.

If you believe that you are, in essence, a steward of your company, then you are responsible for the environment in which your business operates. It is up to you to be aware of the wants and needs of the people who work for you. The goal of the Corporate Samurai is to provide the resources that allow their employees to live richer, fuller lives. To care deeply about these people and to want the very best for them corresponds directly with the spiritual aspects of martial arts.

I continue to teach martial arts part time, and I've come to deeply appreciate something my late Tai Chi teacher once told me.

One day many years ago, he and I were the only people left after our class had ended. We decided to have some tea and went into the back of the school and sat in silence, just honoring the space. I remember looking up and smiling at him. I didn't say anything but felt the warmth emanating from my heart, so grateful to be where I was at that moment of my life.

He smiled back and said, "You know, Ray, all there is, is being together."

I smiled and nodded, not wishing to think about the statement or analyze it in any way.

As the years and decades have passed, never have I heard a more incredible saying.

This, too, fits into our model for the Corporate Samurai.

It's up to you to figure out where and how this statement belongs in your company, family, and life. Read on to gather a few ideas.

I can think of no higher honor than to have individuals look to you for insight into becoming healthier, happier, and more productive human beings who are fully present in their time on earth.

Remember, all there is,
is being together.

Chapter Two: The Makeup of the Enlightened CEO

When I think of the concept of a CEO, the characteristics I envision are charisma, leadership, and strong vision. This is also an adequate description of ANY human being. I think of leaders who are concerned for the welfare of their companies and people. The bottom line is very important because they want to keep their companies profitable. They are strong, supportive, and involved in all phases and departments of their companies. They report to shareholders and to their boards, two entities that measure their results.

In talking with a tremendous number of people who work in corporate America, I've found that very few have even *met* their CEO.

Doesn't this last sentence ring true in your perception of corporate American CEOs?

For most of these CEOs, their *choice of schedule* and *choice of responsibilities* doesn't bring them into contact with the average company worker. Granted, we're probably talking about good-sized companies, but even most employees of medium-sized companies see or communicate very little with their executive management and CEOs. They are usually supervised and nurtured along by their regional director or supervisor.

What has changed over the course of the last several years is most people's view of the corporate CEOs, executive directors, managers, and supervisors who run corporations. The image of the CEO has been greatly tarnished by the corporate scandals that have rocked the business world. Many people now view CEOs as ruthless, rich, power-hungry egomaniacs who will do anything to enhance their bottom line and increase shareholder value. The words honesty, compassion, integrity, and such are not often used in the same sentence as "modern-day CEO."

In some ways, it has never been harder to be a CEO; the media and business world continue to give them a black eye as scandal after scandal shows CEOs on the take, manipulating books and the bottom line—in essence, doing whatever they can to make sure their company's financial statements and P & L look good. It's time to begin healing the battered reputation of the modern-day CEO. However, the CEOs will have to do the work themselves; society and the media won't easily forgive or forget the problems of the past—nor should they.

I would like to provide some concepts, five to be exact, that I feel constitute the healthy makeup of an enlightened CEO: the traits of the Corporate Samurai.

1. LIVING A LIFE OF COMPASSION

Compassion is defined as a sense of shared suffering, most often combined with a desire to alleviate or reduce such suffering.

In my opinion, compassion is one of the most important traits for elevating humans to the next level of evolution. Without compassion, we will continue to focus on our individual needs and desires and give little thought to the person who is in need or who could benefit from what we have to offer.

George Washington Carver made a beautiful and appropriate statement about dealing with compassion. He said, "How far you go in life depends on you being tender with the young,

*Helping people from the depths
of our heart is at the root of
the Samurai philosophy.*

compassionate with the aged, sympathetic with the striving, and tolerant of the weak and the strong. Because someday in life, you will have been all of these."

Our Corporate Samurai is aware that in an ever-changing corporate environment, there will be young (new), aged (experienced), striving (those totally focused on their goals), and weak (those struggling with life issues) employees who will benefit from their CEO's compassion for who they are at that particular time of their life.

Even if you're the CEO of a mid- or large-sized company, you probably don't have the time or the energy to deal with the life issues of most of the people who work for you. However, you can appoint people within human resources or employee relations who can identify potential resources to help your employees. In many situations, you can demonstrate that your company is looking out for your employees, not only through your staff who are hired to help, but also by also providing resources to help in areas the company doesn't specialize in.

I'm not talking about someone in your human resource department handing an employee a card and saying, "Call the EAP (Employee Assistance Program)." I am talking about someone who cares about your employee and the situation he or she is dealing with. When experiencing a difficult life event, it is a wonderful gift to find someone who cares and wants to help resolve the problem as easily and painlessly as possible. Helping people from the depths of our heart is at the root of the Samurai philosophy.

I am reminded of a story I heard concerning the paper executive Charles Schwab.

A paper company paid him the princely sum of $1 million a year to be its executive. He knew that it was largely because of his ability to handle people.

One day, as the story goes, Schwab was touring the plant when he saw several men smoking cigarettes right under a sign that clearly prohibited smoking in that area. The men were nervous as their CEO approached them. Schwab introduced himself to the gentlemen, asked their names, and proceeded to ask them questions about the plant, their jobs, their life at work, and their life at home. He laughed and joked with them as though he was one of them. When it was time to leave, Schwab reached into his jacket and handed each of the men a Cuban cigar. He walked away a few steps and stopped. He turned back, smiled, and said, "Guys, do me a favor. Smoke these *outside*." He winked at them and turned and left.

The men couldn't believe that Schwab would even stop to talk to them, much less offer a gift. When they didn't get chewed out for blatantly breaking the smoking rule, they knew this was an executive who cared about his employees. They were ready to go to war for him. Based on this story, I have no doubt that Schwab understood the value of caring for and nurturing his employees. With a little training, Schwab would make a fabulous Corporate Samurai. Don't you think?

Compassion is a characteristic that we develop by being mindful of caring for other human beings. If I am looking to be compassionate, not one minute goes by in which I cannot show people the compassion I feel for them and their situation. I can think of no better way to connect other individuals than to communicate from the heart that I care about who they are and their goals in life, and that I want to do anything I can to help them do their jobs better, enjoy their life more, or grow as human beings.

If CEOs spent more time looking for ways to help and provide compassionate support to their workers—or in mid- to large size companies, to their department heads—the trickle-down effect would completely shift the company environment. Work quality would increase, and normally shy people would engage others more. People would enjoy their time at work because they would know they were valued from the top down by others who were genuinely concerned about who they are and what was going on in their life.

And let's face it—it feels good down deep in our heart to know that someone is looking out for us in all ways.

The ancient Samurai found compassion in all areas of his life. Compassion can be shown to the simplest life form and can be seen in every act. One can see love and show compassion in the handling of a document, the conversation with a fellow worker, or the frustrations that accompany a missed deadline. Showing compassion allows us to see the depth behind the bottom line. Every Samurai knew and practiced this philosophy.

It is not the goal that important, but the process that leads us along the way.

2. LIVING A LIFE OF INTEGRITY

Integrity is defined as: Moral soundness; honesty; freedom from corrupting influence or motive.[3]

You can see by the above description that a lack of integrity does not go along with the previously discussed compassion. If we are truly looking out for our employees, when and why would we ever not come from a place of the highest integrity?

A woman I know has a film production company and is trying to get her film projects funded and distributed. I met her a few years ago when I was making a film. I had a frightening experience in which our producer and lead actress ran off with the money when the film was only half shot. This woman, whom I'll call Mary, heard my story and agreed to help. I sent her some money to start transferring footage and to prepare the film packages. She became excited when she read other scripts that I was looking to produce. She enthusiastically came on board and took control of fixing my film's problems. Thirty thousand dollars and two and a half years later, the problems still aren't fixed, and she hasn't sent me a single document.

*Deep and authentic compassion
builds a loyalty that is hard to crack.*

Mary talks a great game. She even comes across as completely sincere. When confronted, she always has a great reason why she hasn't sent any material or even returned the footage. It is disturbing to think that people can rationalize any behavior.

Although I've learned some valuable business lessons the painful way, I realize you cannot build a relationship of integrity if you don't have any. Doing what is right for the benefit of others is a wonderful character trait.

Corporate scandals and the guidelines broken by large corporations, as well as the lack of integrity shown by those in charge, have greatly damaged the average person's image of the modern CEO. When CEOs line their pockets and lie to their employees and stockholders while keeping false books, you have the makings of a public disaster that goes far beyond any financial losses. You have a loss of trust, a loss of faith in business, and a loss of faith in the people who run those businesses. Not only do those unscrupulous individuals lose a tremendous amount of respect, but other CEOs, ones who do care about their employees and their business in a healthy way, also take a beating.

The goal is to lead your company by the highest example. I feel that all CEOs should strive to be able to walk down any hallway in their company and know that they are doing right by each person, by the vision of the company, and by their own mission to come from the deepest and best place in their heart to serve not only their company, but the community and world around them.

Let's just summarize in my way what we are building so far:

We have a CEO who is compassionate and who cares deeply about what goes on in the lives of the people who work for the company. This CEO also has high integrity and will look to build the company and its people through solid decision-making and a positive attitude.

Pretty good start, eh?

If you're looking for an example of someone who cares, there are many out there. One person who has inspired me is a gentleman by the name of Paul J. Meyer. Mr. Meyer has built many successful, multi-million-dollar businesses and is famous in his community and the world over for his civic contributions and generosity with his time, energy, and money. Mr. Meyer also lives a spirit-centered life and believes strongly in taking care of those people in his life, whether family or employees.

3. COMMUNICATING WITH HONESTY

The definition of honesty is this: in the context of human communication, people are generally said to be honest when they tell the truth to the best of their knowledge and do not hide what they know or think.

In describing the act of trying to approach life and work from the best and highest possible place, let me share something I heard in a graduate school lecture about humankind's two goals in life. The answer struck me as interesting because the concept seemed so simple, yet when I thought about it, I realized how truly challenging attaining these goals would be. According to this professor, humankind's entire goal is to be *understood and accepted*.

All of humans' goal is to be understood and accepted?

I went away from the lecture puzzled.

There are so many more things that humanity can strive for than these two concepts, I thought driving home.

However, I began to realize the implication of what was said. In order to be *understood*, we have to *understand*. In order to understand ourselves, we have to be willing to look deep within ourselves to see what and who we really are.

Wow!

Most people, I feel, would perceive the statement of being understood and accepted as it applies to how *others understand and accept them.* If you look around, you may often see people trying to "fit in" in many different ways. Clothes, cars, money, and houses are just a few of the materialistic ways people look to gain some measure of acceptance by others. It's not the obvious sort of acceptance, but the illusion of being accepted by our peers in the way we *want* to be perceived. In essence, we provide the energy and the image we want the world to see— not necessarily the most honest and accurate one.

The key here is to understand that before we can truly understand and accept others, we must seek to understand and accept ourselves! I know what I just wrote sounds easy, but if you stop and look deep into your heart and soul, you will realize how truly challenging this can be.

Examining every nook and cranny of our lives, if need be, to discover the depths of who we are can be an amazing yet extremely formidable task. I know few people who have taken or would take the time to do this. It is an ongoing process of continual work and evolution. When you attain understanding at the level you desire, you next work on acceptance. This doesn't seem so hard if you consider that once you understand yourself, it becomes much easier to accept yourself.

This isn't the challenge.

The challenge is honoring self in such a way that you accept yourself to the extent of letting anyone at all ask you questions about your life—in essence, you become the proverbial open book.

Consider another metaphor.

Imagine that your life represents a beautiful throw rug that lies on your floor. It's about eight feet long by four feet wide. Each strand of the rug represents an event in your life. You must have the courage to step out onto your rug and examine every single strand, if need be, to begin to understand who and what you really are and what you're doing here on earth at this time.

Once you've taken the time to discover these insights, you can accept them to such an extent that you could invite anyone onto your rug to inspect, share, and question you. This individual may say something like, "Gee, Ray, look at this spot in the rug. It appears out of whack. What happened here?" I would then walk over, look carefully at what he or she was pointing at, and then share the experience of what that aspect of the rug represented. No fear, no judgment, just the honest experience and feelings that went into that event. This is a different type of honesty—a different type of personal strength. The depth in this encounter creates a tremendous foundation for building trust in a relationship.

Remember our quote about honesty at the beginning of the heading: in the context of human communication, people are generally said to be honest when they tell the truth to the best of their knowledge and do not hide what they know or think.

Truth comes on many different levels. You decide what level you want to come from.

Oprah Winfrey is another individual who comes to mind as someone who appears to care deeply. While I cannot say that I have always agreed with what Oprah has said or done, I have to admire her deeply for her ability to speak her truth and live her life according to what she feels is most important. This is a woman who appears to be very clear in communicating what she wants out of life and goes forward aggressively to achieve it.

You cannot build a relationship of integrity if you don't have any.

Let me briefly review what I just said as it relates to being a Corporate Samurai.

You, as a business owner, manager, CEO, or executive in your company have taken the time to deeply look into the events of your life to get a rich, thorough knowledge of who you are as a human being. Although this is an ongoing process, you have gained a tremendous sense of understanding of your life path, both past and present. You have gained a deeper sense of peace from the process and know what you've worked so hard to become. You've reached such a level of understanding and acceptance that you are willing to share to any depth necessary to help someone understand a situation.

This level of honesty, coupled with heightened integrity and compassion, are foundational blocks that can build a prototype executive the likes of which the world has not yet seen.

But we're not done yet.

4. TO LOVE FROM THE DEPTHS OF OUR HEARTS

Love has many meanings in English, from something that gives a little pleasure ("I loved that movie") to something one would die for (patriotism). It can describe an intense feeling of affection, an emotion, or an emotional state. In ordinary use, it usually refers to interpersonal love. Probably due to its large psychological relevance, love is one of the most common themes in art.

Mother Teresa, incredible woman that she was, gave us some memorable quotes about love.

- Do not think that love, in order to be genuine, has to be extraordinary.
- What we need is to love without getting tired.
- I am not sure exactly what heaven will be like, but I don't know that when we die and it comes time for God to judge us, he will not ask, How many good things have you done in your

Can you become an open book?

People have no trouble turning to you for help, clarification, brainstorming, or insights into anything. The level of understanding of self and acceptance of who you are allows you to present yourself openly and honestly. People are drawn to you like a magnet. The powers wielded by someone who has engaged this process are truly amazing.

Mother Teresa was a Samurai of the highest order.

life? Rather, he will ask, How much love did you put into what you did?

- If we want a love message to be heard, it has got to be sent out. To keep a lamp burning, we have to keep putting oil in it.
- Love begins by taking care of the closest ones—the ones at home.
- Spread love everywhere you go. Let no one ever come to you without leaving happier.

In my opinion, Mother Teresa was one of the most incredible people to ever walk the planet. She changed the world through her selfless acts for her fellow human. In my opinion, that's the epitome of love and compassion. She did not seek out to create a mega billion-dollar empire; rather, she chose to devote her existence to easing suffering and helping those who needed it most.

Although she founded the organization Missionaries of Charity, she never deviated from her goal of being hands-on in helping the suffering people of the world. Her goal was not to sit in an executive board room and raise money for her own gain. Inspired by her example, people joined her in the battle to ease the world's suffering.

Mother Teresa provides the highest example I can think of, of someone who came from the deepest place in her heart to help those who needed it. Her actions arose from the love in her heart for all people, not from materialism or ego or from a need for recognition, or fame. They arose from a desire to help and serve.

The traditional Samurai experienced love on many different levels. One of their greatest gifts was the ability to love and appreciate everything *in the moment*. Samurai could love and appreciate a sunset, the falling of the blossom as it drifted lazily from the tree, the simple smile of a child. Love comes from the deep desire to be connected to everything that surrounds us—to be connected as one. This love and awareness of life itself, in all its manifestations, is at the root of the Samurai philosophy.

By no means am I asking anyone to provide the level of commitment to love and care for those in need of Mother Teresa. *Or am I?*

5. KEEPING THE HEALTHIEST VISION IN FOCUS

Visionary: the person in the organization who articulates the direction—what is intended to be accomplished.

What motivates and inspires people in an organization is a vision that they can get behind. However, it is one thing to get behind a company vision that everyone can support; it is quite another to get behind someone who has the tools and character to create a vision *for each person.*

There have been numerous incredible visionaries throughout time. Great minds like Albert Einstein, Leonardo da Vinci, and Buckminster Fuller are just a few examples of people who stretched their minds to discover new boundaries in consciousness and the physical universe. Someone in the present who comes to mind as fitting in this group is Deepak Chopra. Dr. Chopra has pushed very hard and is doing an incredible job of tying the science of quantum physics to modern views of spirituality.

New ideas and innovative methods are what drive evolution. If we are not willing to push to improve our current condition, by definition we will exist in a stagnant environment. Our current corporate climate is in just such a state. We have been working from the bottom-line model far too long, and an economic, cultural, and consciousness shift must take place before we can reach the next level of evolved business.

The Corporate Samurai will be such a step. These new executives will not only be connected to the financial stability of the company, they will also be closely aware of the people who serve them and whom they serve. "Serve" is the operative word. From the Samurai perspective, coming from a place of service is the highest level of existence.

The Samurai lived their lives to serve the greater good. So do the modern-day Corporate Samurai.

You, as a modern-day Corporate Samurai, will provide a level of honesty and integrity that will redefine corporate America as well as your life. You will come from the deepest place in your being to connect with those you work with and provide as much opportunity for growth, development, and creativity as possible. You will push the vision of your company past the point of worrying about financial solvency and move to the higher level of service as dictated by the needs of your communities and the drive, commitment, and interest of your employees. The money will be a foregone conclusion, as this level of efficiency will provide a perfect matrix to allow the money to flow.

As your company's Corporate Samurai, you will be the heart and soul of your company's engine. Everything will flow from you at the top. When you, the CEO, are balanced, centered, rooted in deep compassion, and driven to provide the best you can for all your employees, your company will not only be solvent and profitable, it will *explode* in all phases of business. Job satisfaction will skyrocket, and employees will connect on a deeper level with one another in their professional and personal lives. The working environment will shift from one of forced performance to the excitement of wishing to contribute.

People not only want to work for a company like the one we've described, but your average, everyday consumer will want to buy from this type of company! We are all looking for people who come from the best place in their heart and take care of everyone around them in all ways that are important to them.

And if we can't work for them, we'll be involved somehow, even if all we can do is be customers. New CEOs, directors, executives, and business owners will create a new style of doing business that will change the fabric of our economy.

A couple of years ago, I had a meeting with the minister of the church my family attends. Our minister, David McArthur, is a Unity Minister and former lawyer. David is one of the most amazing souls I have ever met; his life knowledge combined with his knowledge of spiritual principles is truly amazing. Beyond that, he is simply one of the warmest, most compassionate men I have ever known.

I wanted to share with him the conceptual philosophy of three companies I was proposing. I told him my idea for a film company called We R One Productions. I have always been interested in film, stories, acting, and drama and wanted to make commercial yet inspirational films that crossed over different genres. I had some scripts, experiences—both good and bad—and desire. I also had the business plan for a new software company that will dramatically change education and business. The third company is a design model that will provide opportunities never before offered to at-risk youth.

I brought to David the idea of sharing the physical and spiritual gifts that I believed these companies represented. I shared my visions of the companies for about half an hour while he listened intently. At the end of my description, I asked, "Does that sound to you to be rooted in spiritual service and prosperity for all?"

He smiled enthusiastically. "Ray, these companies sound wonderful. The service and opportunities to help mankind are amazing," he said with heartfelt warmth.

I smiled; I knew he understood what I was trying to do. Then I took a step further. "Do you know of anyone who is more connected in the business world than I am, as I don't travel much in large, affluent circles?"

You, as a modern-day Corporate Samurai, will provide a level of honesty and integrity that will redefine corporate America as well as your life.

"I believe I know just such a man," David said with a hint of a smile.

Shortly thereafter, David and I were on a flight to L.A. I had prepared a business plan and Power Point presentation about our software company for this gentleman to view. My minister thought that we should start with that company, as it had the most detailed business plan and its potential impact is global.

I walked this gentleman and David through the presentation and let him peruse the business plan for about ten minutes.

"This company is one of the companies I'm most excited about, as the potential to help people of all ages is tremendous," I offered as he set the business plan back down onto the table.

He looked at me quizzically. "What do you mean *one* of the companies?"

Right then, David smiled and spoke up.

"Ray, let's stay focused on *this* company."

"No, no. Tell me," the gentleman said with a contagious smile. "You have other ideas? Let me hear."

I looked back at David, who shrugged and smiled.

I then proceeded to talk about our youth-development model, called Steps for Life, which focuses on providing work, training, mentoring, and whatever young people need for the next step. It's a wonderful model that is sorely needed in today's world.

I quickly transitioned into a brief description of our film company, We R One Productions. I told him that this company was designed to make commercially viable, exciting, transformational films that take universal spiritual principles and weave

People not only want to work for a company like the one we've described, but your average, everyday consumer will want to buy from this type of company!

them into the films' content. In the end, when audiences come out of the theater, not only will they have been entertained, but they will also leave with some new ideas to consider. I followed this up with a description of a new software application that could affect millions of people in an incredibly positive way.

Half an hour later, he turned to David and said, "Where have you been hiding this fellow?"

David could only smile as I felt the joy in my heart exploding.

This gentleman then shared with us his vision for helping the planet and his desire to build an infrastructure that would support any business structure one would want. This gentleman had the framework, or engine, to wrap around any business to create traction and interest. His skills in fundraising and marketing were beyond anything I had ever seen. His goal to help transform the planet was not only inspiring but intoxicating as well.

We left for lunch and continued our conversation. At lunch, we agreed to work together an even got the restaurant to let us borrow a room, pens, and a flip chart as we began fleshing out the details of our software program.

I left that day elated and stunned. My vision for helping to transform the planet and assisting people had been heard and embraced by someone with an equally powerful vision. In fact, the connections and knowledge this gentleman had went light years beyond my scope of knowledge in business. We continue to this day, growing and expanding our strategic alliance as more and more people come forward who wish to be a part of this amazing process.

The wonderful Stephen Covey wrote in *The Seven Habits of Highly Successful People* that one of the habits is beginning with the end in mind.[4] Envision yourself and your company as you would dream them to be at their highest level of functionality and sustainability.

Even though the ancient Samurai perpetually focused on the moment, they were fully aware of the direction in which their lives were moving. Their vision encompassed peace and prosperity for their own village and province, and for the entire country and world as well.

I see the world as full of hopes, dreams, possibilities, and opportunities to help others. I've committed my life to this process. I will push my heart, mind, and vision to come together and *play* in an arena that is about business, consciousness, service, and opportunity for everyone. More and more people are coming on board who also are deeply affected by this vision. As more and more people come on board our companies, the vision widens and deepens as the universe continually pours forth its gifts.

As we move forward, new visionary CEOs like the Corporate Samurai will elevate the working environment that binds us closer together, unifying dreams and personal aspirations and creating a model for others in business to follow. By taking care of our business and the people within it, we are setting a standard for care and compassion that will transfer over into *all* business models.

Don't take my word for it. Sit and ponder what you have read and don't analyze it; just sit with it in your heart and see if the still, small voice inside you doesn't enthusiastically agree about the merits of this model and send warm thoughts that resonate deeply within you.

Listen to the amazing wisdom of your heart. By following that wisdom, you will uncover a whole new way of gathering information and knowledge that did not and does not come from a lecture or textbook.

If we don't see it in our minds and hearts, if we don't put it out to the universe, *nothing will happen.*

Compassion, integrity, honesty, loving from the depths, and having a strong vision. Whether you are the actual CEO or not, everyone can strive to live from the qualities of compassion, integrity, honesty, loving from the depths, and having a strong personal vision.

Don't you think?

The Samurai were unfailingly conscious of their vision of a better world for all.

A wonderful fire will start that will spread as more and more enlightened CEOs discover the true path of business.

Chapter Three: The Role of the Enlightened CEO: Steward

Stewardship: Taking responsibility for the survival and well-being of something that is valued.

In the previous chapter, we looked at the characteristics that make up the Corporate Samurai. Compassion, honesty, integrity, love, and vision were the five traits that we identified as being vital in reaching this new level of administrative success. At best, without these traits, the organization will flounder like a ship with no rudder. At worst, the organization will be damaging to its employees and to everyone and everything it comes into contact with.

By bringing the five qualities mentioned above into the makeup of our CEOs, we will be cultivating an environment that will transform the company in every way. CEOs, executive directors, managers, and business owners are *stewards* over their companies.

Again, doesn't this definition fit perfectly in our model?

Most CEOs are concerned primarily about the survival of what they value: the company. I believe, deep in my heart, that most people truly want to care about the well-being of their employ-

Never forget:
The corporate environment has to
do with not only the physical and
emotional space of your company, but
also the social, mental, financial, and
spiritual components of your space.

ees. However, a desire to care about employees and actually doing something about are two different things. Most CEOs are focused on sustainability and profit—i.e., the bottom line.

In this chapter I'd like you to consider some concepts about the Corporate Samurai within.

THE CORPORATE OR BUSINESS ENVIRONMENT

When people think of their corporate or work environment, they usually think of the physical and emotional space where they work.

I'd like to expand that to include everything *in between.*

The corporate environment has to do with not only the physical and emotional space of your company, but also the social, mental, financial, and spiritual components of your space.

You may be thinking, "Uh-oh, here comes that word—*spiritual.*"

Don't run.

I hate to break this to you, but *every* corporate environment fits into some type of a spiritual model and can be seen within a spiritual framework.

Think of it as a one-to-ten scale. A "one" indicates that the word "spirit" is rarely if ever used. When it is used, it is usually during coffee or lunch breaks, away from the "eye" of the company. People may talk about spirituality with their close co-workers, but rarely does this topic leave that safe haven.

A "ten" represents a company that is *led* by what I refer to as Spirit. What I mean is that this type of company looks to Spirit for guidance and seeks inspiration through the still, small voice within. This voice can be found in the quiet mind often associated with prayer or meditation. This guidance, while not popular in the mainstream, is an amazingly powerful tool. Employees of such a company are guided and empowered by Spirit and trust that the truest source of the good in their lives comes from Spirit. While they may not use one term like "God" or "Jesus," they may use terms like Spirit, Creative Consciousness, or any number of other descriptions that represent the spiritual aspect that they feel guides them.

This is the key.

Too many times we hear a word or a name and associate it with something that may have nothing to do with the pure spiritual principle. For example, look at the feelings that come up when you think of the word "politics." Many people may experience images and memories they associate with dishonest, lying politicians who said whatever they needed to say in order to get elected. But when I listen to what my heart and spirit say about the concept of "politics," I experience a feeling of deep trust, care, and the idea that someone is looking out for me, my family, and our best interests. I want to feel deeply in my heart that our politicians possess the highest level of integrity and care. The mention of Dr. Martin Luther King brings up a lot of images for a lot of people. For most, he symbolizes the Civil Rights movement of the '60s, when he spoke passionately about coming together as one people, united in our human heritage. There are still people who view Dr. King as someone who "stirred up" problems and that he should have left well enough alone.

Thousands of years of judgment and persecution are associated with the concept of spirituality. I can't think of more *charged* words than "religion" or "spirituality." The at-risk young people I work with find it fascinating that the human race wiped out millions of people because of their own inability to honor the spiritual beliefs of others. We in America have the freedom to express our thoughts and to believe in a god of our own choosing. Billions of people in the world still cannot freely worship the spiritual powers that they wish. The practice of pulling spirituality out of our education is reaching worrisome proportions. Religion, I can understand, but spirituality—*never*.

Don't get me wrong. I'm not an advocate who will show people "The Way."

I do not believe there is only *one* way.

The *way* is what works for people—period.

I remember a story my grandmother told me when I was a child about honoring other people's path. She said that it is everyone's goal to get to the top of the mountain and we all start out from the same place at the bottom and begin climbing. We move onward and upward as we travel the mountain paths. Friends join in, and we find ourselves walking along with others who wish to travel the same path. As we travel, guides come forth to help us find our way to the top. Sometimes we part ways with our friends as they follow another path.

Along the way, we meet up with others on the path, and sometimes we try to convince each other that *our path is best*.

We sometimes leave disappointed and angry and throw rocks at the other people for making a "dumb" choice.

However, we should stop and realize that the only goal is to reach the top of the mountain, and as long as we never stop ascending, the path we take doesn't matter—as long as it resonates within us.

I remember thinking how wise my grandmother was, despite some of the stories I heard about her when she was young. She wasn't always the most centered, spiritual person in the room. She had lived a full life and had come a long way in honoring other people and their views.

With that said, I do believe there are certain universal principles inherent in all spiritual traditions. Concepts like hon-

Our culture has become afraid to openly discuss spirituality—afraid that they may not be "politically correct" or they may be offending someone by speaking about religion. This creates hesitancy, at best, to share our personal spiritual views.

esty, compassion, integrity, service, and love ... hmm, sound familiar?

It's funny that although I am an ordained Interfaith Minister, I do not consider myself religious at all. I believe myself to be very *spiritual*, and I am in constant contact with Spirit—but *religious*? Nope.

When certain Christians hear something about the Buddha and Buddhism, quickly their defenses go up in resistance, as it is something different than what they grew up believing. Some people watch a Native American dance and wonder about the strangeness of it.

I'm suggesting that we as Corporate Samurai honor all paths and that we can use very spiritual words—like compassion, love, honesty, integrity, service, and vision—to create a very spiritual, yet not religious environment.

How do we do that?

We begin by asking questions about the above topics as they relate to our environment or the environment we envision, questions like:

> In what ways do we verbally show compassion to our employees?
> In what ways do we physically show compassion to our employees?
> In what ways do we mentally show compassion to our employees?
> In what ways do we emotionally show compassion to our employees?
> In what ways do we socially show compassion to our employees?
> In what ways do we spiritually show compassion to our employees?
> In what ways do we financially show compassion to our employees?

You don't have to preach a certain gospel to come from a spiritual framework.

These seven questions can be asked for each of the topics identified in the previous chapter: honesty, compassion, integrity, love, and vision. These questions can be modified and changed in order to flush out what it is you want to discover and provide as a Corporate Samurai. These are great questions to brainstorm about with your employees, who will come up with wonderful ideas for ways to provide the best you can for them.

When you ask this type of question to your employees, you will get a clear and deep sense of what these topics sound, look, and feel like *to them*. Find out what thoughts and ideas about how these topics could be manifested within your company.

These are not only questions one can ask in their company, but also questions that can be asked at home and in their personal life. You can ask all of these questions in each of these areas to your family and friends. The true Samurai lives a consistent life and takes every relationship to heart.

STAFF

We've provided a starting point for your company to begin looking at the traits of the Corporate Samurai. Now, I'd like to narrow our focus and look at some deeper questions that may be addressed to the individuals within the company.

One of the greatest gifts you can give employees is the gift of care and concern for health, welfare, and safety—of not only the employees themselves, but their families as well. If I knew in my heart that my employer was truly concerned about my and my family's well-being, I would feel blessed to have this type of relationship with my company.

Imagine if the company you worked for was willing to invest the time to come to know you as a human being, to find out the details of your life and what drives you, and then to provide heartfelt suggestions and resources to help you fulfill your goals. What kind of a difference would that make in your view of the company? If you share the depths of yourself with your employees or employer (depending on which role applies), and if this person were to honor what you said and hold it close to his or her heart, I would think that one couldn't help but feel closer to this person.

That kind of honoring and acceptance would allow you to feel better about your honesty and help deepen your understanding of yourself and what you are doing in the world. Once you are on this path and feeling good, your personal growth would naturally flow outward to others. In essence, you would be getting back to the goals of *understanding and accepting*. Only now, your willingness to open up and share has created potentially incredible returns as your relationship with your employer, employees, and family, as well as your own life, will become deeper and more honest. Characteristics described in the Corporate Samurai model come to the surface, and it becomes much easier to continue this process.

I'd like to offer five areas to consider when coming from the best place in your heart in supporting your employees and encouraging this process of growing, both as individuals and as companies. They are:

> *Health*
> *Finances*
> *Relationships*
> *Career or Creative Expression*
> *Personal and Spiritual Growth*

There may be other areas you would like to include, but these are the main ones I would suggest you begin with. Feel free to add additional areas as you feel the need.

I would ask you to consider offering a visioning exercise in each of these areas. This is a wonderful activity to do with your employees, and you will be amazed at the positive energy that will come simply from offering the exercise! An example of the exercise may simply be to have your employees close their eyes and relax. Once relaxed, ask them how they would ide-

Remember: Caring for your employees is a wonderful thing. Caring for the family of your employees puts you on a whole new Samurai level.

ally like to see the specific area of their lives. Document the answers.

HEALTH

Allow the employees to consider the questions below and create their vision of optimum health. It is important to take your time when visioning, as this sets the quantum universe in motion to begin creating a new reality. Encourage the group to vision using all of their senses—to see the colors, smell the fragrances, feel the texture, hear the words.... Allow the senses to fully embrace the questions and the answers.

> *What would optimum physical health look like for you?*
> *How would your body look different?*
> *How would you move differently?*
> *What would optimum emotional health look like for you?*
> *If you were in wonderful health, how would that change the words you chose to speak?*
> *How would your perspective on life change if you were even more emotionally healthy than you are now?*
> *What would optimum mental health look like for you?*
> *Would your relationships change? If they would change, how?*

It is important to allow each person to create his or her own vision. It is also important to be able to stimulate this type of thinking. If an employee has difficulty *seeing* optimum health, she may benefit from you sharing a vision of a component of optimum health. Sometimes people just need a little help or push to get them going.

Document the answers to these questions. The answers will provide the tools necessary to a Corporate Samurai to develop contacts and resources that will aid your employees in achieving their goals. You will be able to see your employees' common ground and then begin connecting the pieces by providing the resources or programs that address the needs of your company.

It is not imperative that you as the CEO provide the answers. It may be enough to provide the professional resources or referrals to help guide employees farther down their path.

FINANCES

Finances are a large part of people's lives. Living comfortably by having an adequate supply of money is very important to most people. It has been my experience that the worry and struggle in people's lives revolve more around money than any other issue.

Financial support—paying employees well enough that they can live comfortably and have their needs met—is an interesting concept. While we realize that financial freedom would enhance our lives by removing our stress or worry about money, we realize that having enough money is only *part* of the process that enables us to achieve our deepest sense of balance. Having said that, it is very important to have money in our lives because it alleviates our fears and provides for us, our children, and our retirements. Beyond that, a consciousness of prosperity and philanthropy is another level of financial freedom that enhances our lives even more. Money is a tool to be used in many ways to gain the things we desire in life. We may trust that money is like water in that it can easily flow through lives. Hoarding money does nothing to increase the flow. We can choose to allow money to continually flow through lives, and we can use money to not only gain what we want in our lives, but also in the lives of others. To be able to give to others for causes that we deem important is one of the great experiences of life.

As with everything we are discussing concerning this enlightened Samurai model, striking a balance is the key.

Once again, during the visioning exercise, allow the employees to visualize and begin to discover the areas of finance that they wish to create or modify.

Questions might include:

What would financial wealth look like and feel like to you?

What financial goals must be achieved for you to be happy now? Ten years from now? Twenty years from now?

What types of things would you hear if you experienced a wonderful increase in financial prosperity?

How would vacations change?

Would food taste different if there were no money worries?

How and when do you see yourself retiring?

What type of financial support do you want to provide for your children?

Again, document the answers.

You may wish to provide as much financial support as possible for your employees. This may take the shape of promotional opportunities or job enrichment programs. The potential is limitless.

It is not imperative that you as the CEO provide the answers. It may be enough to provide the professional resources or referrals to help guide employees farther down their path to financial prosperity. The goal is to *help*. By helping, you are demonstrating that you are aware of and sympathetic to employees' needs and desires. If you can help foster a consciousness about prosperity and philanthropy in your employees, then you have truly done your job.

RELATIONSHIPS

Relationships can make or break someone's experience at work. You can make great money, but if you are not getting along with anyone in the company, then how are you truly grow-

The Samurai knows that relationships that are nurtured and honored grow into friendships with the strongest and deepest roots.

ing and enjoying the career you've invested so much time and money in?

My wife has worked for over twenty years in the dental laboratory field. For the majority of those years she has worked in an environment that was less than what she had hoped for. The lab owners did not believe in talking at work unless it was about the particular case they were working on. Not only were employees not allowed to talk, they were not allowed to listen to music during the course of the day, as the owner felt that this would distract them from their work.

Wow! Pretty scary, huh?

Most people are social by nature and greatly benefit from social interaction and companionship while at work. Granted, you can't allow your friendliness to interfere with your work productivity, but the ability to have meaningful and healthy social relationships at work is vital to each employee's mental and emotional health.

The Samurai viewed relationships as vital to personal and spiritual growth, in that we use the experiences from our relationships to grow and learn from. We find that our deepest joys come from the relationships we've invested the most time in. The close relations kept by the Samurai to the people in their villages were strong enough that the Samurai would lay down their lives for their people. Relationships are among the Samurai's most treasured gifts.

This seems to have drastically changed in today's modern world of high-rolling CEOs. The depth of the relationships the CEO has with most of his or her employees is on the surface level—at best!

Most CEOs don't take the time to discover anything more than the basics needed to qualify employees for work, instruct them in their job, and reveal their compensation package. Employees may occasionally get a brief conversation with the CEO as they're asked if you watched the football game the other night. The relationship goes about that deep.

Remember the phrase: All there is, is being together.

During the visioning process, ask the questions:

How do you want your relationships with others to feel at work and at home?

If you could change something about your relationship with a co-worker, what would you want to change?

If you could change something about your relationship with a family member, what would you want to shift?

If you could change something about your relationship with one of your friends, what changes would you make?

Allow time to let the insights surface. Gently honor the wisdom that comes. Remember to document and make the appropriate changes as needed.

CAREER OR CREATIVE EXPRESSION

As we all know, our career is one of the most important and time-consuming activities in which we will ever engage. Too many people are involved in jobs and careers that they are not connected to or passionate about. The Corporate Samurai recognizes the need to provide opportunities to not only discover, but to engage employees through job enhancement and training, enabling them to fulfill their ultimate destiny. The Samurai looks for way to stimulate his people. This is investing in the *total person* and not a limited asset that can easily be replaced.

Sometimes, employers and CEOs take the opposite tack. They purposely keep the employee focused and limited on completing a small range of tasks. They often feel that if the employee gains more marketable skills, he or she would leave and seek employment elsewhere.

For years, my wife wanted to learn the dental laboratory skills necessary to be a porcelain stacker and grinder. Her employee refused to share this skill with my wife. In the end, she felt unappreciated and unsupported. She left and went to work in a lab with a much more open mindset. Sadly, her previous employer continues to treat its employees as limited, expendable assets. Consequently, they have employees who don't stick around long, and the environment continues to be toxic.

In creating a positive environment that allows people to grow and develop and enhance their creativity, one may ask questions like:

> *What do you want to express and create in your professional life?*

> *What do you want to express and create in your personal life?*

> *What support would you need from us, the company, in helping you create these things?*

I've always felt that if a company has the need and an employee has the drive and desire to work in that need, you have a potential match made in heaven. Both the company and employee will benefit from allowing employees to broaden their career skills by taking on a new challenge. By supporting the employee through training, encouragement, and constant positive feedback, the company creates an environment in which the employees learn that *anything is possible* and that they, too, can grow in a way that not only serves the company but also allows for personal, creative expression.

This builds security and deep loyalty.

As with all areas previously discussed, allow the vision to take shape. This is something that can take time and may also benefit from the support of fellow employees. The concept of nurturing and stimulating employees to be creative in their personal and professional lives will gain in popularity as more and more employees and employers see its incredible value.

Take notes and discuss with your employee and your team of resources options to help manifest this reality. Your employees will not only appreciate the ability to discuss this process, their level of appreciation will deepen as the commitment they feel from the company in supporting their goals also deepens.

PERSONAL AND SPIRITUAL GROWTH

Consider this: in the past twenty-four hours, nearly half of your employees have talked about their faith at work. That may seem surprising, but it's true, according to a *Business Week* poll of March 14, 2003. In their book *Spiritual Audit of Corporate America* Ira Mitroff and Elizabeth Denton state:

> We believe that the workplace is one of the most important settings in which people come together daily to accomplish what they cannot do on their own, that is, to realize their full potential as human beings. For organizations to erect walls in the way of everyday spiritual development goes against the grain of deep human needs and puts an intolerable burden on individuals. Unless organizations become more spiritual, the fragmentation and ambivalence felt by individuals cannot be repaired. [5]

It is clear that allowing spiritual awareness into corporate America is gaining momentum. An awareness of a concept is one thing—taking the necessary spiritual steps that honor and provide support in the most fulfilling way for all concerned is another. The evolving nature of spirituality is making its way into all facets of our lives. According to a March 14, 2003 poll, Business Wire stated that the majority of adults believe spirituality at work is beneficial. Incorporating spirituality with work

Remember: unless organizations become more spiritual, the fragmentation and ambivalence felt by individuals cannot be repaired.

is a huge step in bringing our companies, cities, and planet to a deeper state of peace. [6]

In all areas previously discussed, I have talked about the ability to care and to provide the best we can to help our employees discover things of great meaning in their life. We've looked at their health from different angles, their financial goals, inter-personal relationships, and the desire to create within their careers. All of the topics we've discussed fit under the area of personal growth. And personal growth, whether it be personal, professional, or spiritual, is a concept we must explore to enhance the potential within our company.

It is important to be aware of and careful about one's choice of language when discussing spirituality. Our corporate climate is such that political correctness has hit new levels. Having anyone come up to you and dump his or her religious doctrine upon you makes you uncomfortable at best. Having a co-worker who constantly goes around spouting religious text is not something most of us would enjoy. If that person, by chance, happens to focus on you and your life and then begins trying to "fix" things, well, now you're in for more fun. Very few people like being lectured on the Ten Commandments and what is right and wrong in their life.

Let me be clear: I am not advocating any type of religious ceremony or discussing beliefs or even opinions in the work environment. What I am suggesting is the ability to discuss is what I call universal spiritual principles. These are concepts that revolve around one's meaning and purpose; living an honest, integrity-filled life that serves the greater good; and loving and caring about our family and friends.

Does this sound familiar?

What we just described was the structure and living philosophy of the Samurai. It is spiritual.

It does not have to be religious.

Don't be afraid to take on the concept of spirituality. It's here to stay and is gaining momentum.

When speaking about *spirituality*, I would suggest you offer a question that will allow the employee to help you understand this important element. The questions might be something like this:

What qualities do you see in your spiritual life?

What spiritual qualities would you like to see in your personal life?

What spiritual qualities would you like to see in your professional life?

How would you like to see these qualities integrated in both your personal and professional lives?

Allow the vision to sink into the consciousness of your employees. You may be amazed at what universal spiritual principles your employees agree upon. Once you have discussed and documented their answers, begin the process of discovering the vast multitude of ways you and your company can become aware of and demonstrate spiritual principles. In no time at all, your business environment will shift to one of compassion, integrity, and a deep sense of connection and team spirit. The concept of "work" will shift, and the enjoyment, fulfillment, and quality of work will skyrocket.

True Samurai see the Spirit in all things. While the Samurai's religious beliefs may have been rooted in Buddhism, their focus was on what are they doing *in the moment.* Their lives revolved around how could they better live, love, and serve.

Remember, one does not need to be a martial arts master to walk the way of the Samurai. However, to walk the way of a Corporate Samurai takes courage and integrity few people in life, let alone in business, have dared to embrace. The reward for this act of bravery is a level of peace and happiness rooted in the knowledge that you have done the very best you could to honor your business, its mission, and its employees.

Don't be afraid; this is the purest, greatest, most heart-centered path I can imagine. The rewards you reap will surprise and astound you; every area of your life will improve.

A well-lived, meaningful existence in the cut-throat world of business is rare.

The fact of the matter is that most CEOs are afraid.

That's right, they're afraid.

CEOs have been trained to look at business from a matter-of-fact perspective. They weren't taught to look into the very depths of their own soul and seek out the Samurai within. Being trained to show compassion and love for their employees while developing a healthy vision for all was not in their college curriculum. Most, if given the chance, would say it's not necessary and business is business and getting personal doesn't belong in the boardroom.

They are speaking from their fear of change and about a model with which they are not familiar.

Most CEOs, or anyone for that matter, are not trained in the way of the Samurai.

It is not to say CEOs and people in general don't have wonderful gifts – they do. However, think about a professional tennis player. No player who ever got to the top ever got their without training and support. Now more than ever is there a need to train CEOs and people in general in the ways of the Samurai.

CHAPTER FOUR:
ENLIGHTENED EXPANSION

We've spent the previous pages identifying reasons why businesses may exist, the characteristics that make up the Corporate Samurai, and the role that they play. We've examined the role of the new CEO and how important it is to consider not only the health and welfare of the business by looking out for employees in the richest ways possible, we've stressed concepts that will take the business model to new levels.

So what is the next step when a business agrees on the need to create a new environment based on the principles discussed? What next? Do you hire a consultant and trainer to come in and help restructure the environment? Maybe. Do you sit down with your existing employees and executives and discuss the merits of such a cultural shift?

Absolutely.

Expand the circle of success by, first of all, agreeing to embrace the concepts that shift from the goal of only looking at the *bottom line* to one that looks at the health and welfare of the organization from the Corporate Samurai model. You'll still be concerned with the financial growth of the company but you'll be broadening your focus to begin looking at the quality of your organization and its people. This starts with you, the CEO of your business and life. Once you have agreed upon a

Be willing to shift from the goal of only looking at the bottom line to one that looks at the health and welfare of the people and the organization from the Corporate Samurai model.

plan, either discuss within the organization or hire a consultant to help you bridge the gap in this transition.

Once the transition is made, work hard at honoring the mission of the business and the commitment to each and every employee. Continue to strive to improve the quality of care and services that you provide not only to your clients but to your employees as well. See them as the extended family that has bought into the vision of your company and the direction they are choosing to go. Honor them from the deepest place in your heart, and do right by them in the way you would pray that others do right by you. We will only change the world as we are willing to change first ourselves, then our business philosophy.

This expansion takes the form of personal transformation that must begin in those in charge. The Corporate Samurai's leadership begins and ends with executive management. Once management buys into the philosophy, it must commit itself to fulfill, to the best of its abilities, the principles agreed upon. Teams will be constructed to carefully review and recommend appropriate changes to bring the milieu into its new state of enlightenment.

What could be better?

STRATEGIC ALLIANCE

Now that you have your new organizational philosophy in place and are walking the talk, it may be time to expand. I'm not necessarily talking about opening another branch, outlet, or office. I'm talking about expanding with the right people, in the right environment, with the right philosophy that resonates with yours.

In Cyrus Freidheim's book *The Trillion-Dollar Enterprise: How the Alliance Revolution Will Transform Global Business,* Freidman says that for businesses to expand and see their highest potential, they must create strategic partnerships that benefit each organization involved. These organizations join to form coalitions that dominate their industries. This new style of strategic alliance, coupled with the business philosophy of the Corporate Samurai, provides a blueprint for success never before seen in business economics. [7]

The idea of taking a good concept, product, or service and making it into a business can be, and often is, a logical and beneficial addition to communities. Creating a business with the philosophy of the Corporate Samurai takes business and employee relations to another level entirely. If we take this model and expand it by growing the business and creating additional companies or aligning with appropriate strategic partners, we now have a model of doing business that is not only run from the heart and consciousness of the Samurai, but is also expanding and including others in its mission. This creates the potential for a planetary shift in business management and philosophy.

Understand, Freidman and I are not talking of giving up your existing company. We're talking about forming an alliance with another company that shares your goals and vision; the strength of each company helps build the other. Each company is strengthened by the agreement to work together and provide products or services. I know this is something virtually every CEO in the country knows. I'm asking you to consider what you as a company want to contribute to society.

This model constantly asks the questions that allow for honest reflection, personal growth, authentic and honest communication, and the ability to serve everyone who comes into contact with our organization at the highest level. It means going the extra mile in providing the very best we can in every way possible.

Honestly speaking, I have *never* seen a company do this.

In sharing my ideas with colleagues and friends in the business world, they agree that the model is incredible—idealistic, but incredible. It's time.

The following questions are a few to consider when evaluating the potential to expand using strategic alliances:

Are we interested in expansion, and if so, to what extent do we wish to expand?

Who is out there who may be interested in helping this expansion?

What do we have to gain by expanding with another company that we've identified?

What does the other company have to gain by expanding with us?

How does this expansion best serve the mission of our company?

How does this expansion best serve the employees of both companies?

If in answering these questions you come up with a list of positives for both you and the other company, then it may well benefit both of your companies to discuss the merits of such an alliance. This process allows companies to strengthen themselves and expand in a way that creates a new entity that serves the community. This process can and has been done with literally dozens of companies coming together to form entities that grow and dominate their markets.

If you see a particular niche that you wish to create by aligning with a strategic partner and you don't see a company out there that resonates with you, *create your own*. Don't be afraid to create another business entity that aligns with your present one.

The Corporate Samurai model mandates that we continually reexamine where we are, where we want to go, who we're serving, and why.

I, along with my partner, have a youth-development model we're about to launch that provides wonderful opportunities for all concerned. We will provide education, work experience, training for young men and young women who truly need it. We have already formed the existing corporate structure, but we will also be creating several other corporate structures to support this company. In this way, we can drive business to ourselves by using the new company for services that we would normally farm out to other corporate structures. Things like human resources, equipment leases, and payroll are just a few of the areas that we can leverage to create more jobs, greater prosperity, and more opportunities for everyone involved.

I call this the Corporate Family.

This structure can grow in so many different ways. Not only can you provide more and more products and services to the community, under your Corporate Samurai leadership, you become a stronger and more aware member of your community. By providing the kind of environment discussed in this book, and by allowing yourself, if you desire, to expand with well-considered strategic alliances, you are creating a healthy, enlightened empire.

This can be an amazingly powerful organization.

This Corporate Family can do a tremendous amount of good not only in your community, but beyond. Not only does it create a new model to emulate, it provides a standard of growth and employee relations that literally draw people to its light. The energy that this organization puts off will be one of service, honor, integrity, and social awareness. This is where we're headed.

A wonderful example of this type of organization is Doctors Without Borders. This entity is an independent, international, medical humanitarian organization that delivers emergency aid to people in nearly sixty countries who have been affected by armed conflict, epidemics, natural or man-made disasters, or exclusion from health care. A great model of giving for all of us to emulate!

We can choose to stay in the "old-school" model that uses people in a limited way, focuses only on the bottom line, and does nothing to evolve the consciousness of the planet. These organizations employ people who feel stuck in their jobs and feel stagnant in their lives. The only ones who typically gain in this model are the owners of the corporation or business, and they generally only gain financially. These types of leaders are often cut off from their employees and disconnected from their employees' needs. This does not breed loyalty, happiness, or fulfillment within anyone in the organization.

Or, we can choose to embrace the reality we know in our heart—one of honoring and caring deeply for those who we are privileged to serve: our employees and our customers.

We will be providing a model of community ethics by being aware of the needs of ourselves, our employees, and beyond that, the needs of the community. This is transformation. This is the path to enlightenment. It comes by way of service, love, integrity, and honor. It walks a path clear in purpose and is open of heart. It honors those it serves and those who serve with it. It knows no higher purpose than to come from the deepest place in the heart and to serve all who come into contact with the organization.

This is the path of the Corporate Samurai. It leads to love, success, and business enlightenment. It is a model of transformation to be explored and molded to fit each business that wishes to forge a new path to success.

Engage in the process.

By looking to take care of our employees while creating stability and sustainability in our business, we will be cultivating an environment of growth and success on every level that has meaning.

Spirituality is found in the awareness we choose in each and every moment, recognizing that the Divine Intelligence that created everything is part of our very essence—that we are connected to that intelligence.

Chapter Five: The Legacy

There have been many books in the last few years advocating a changing philosophy in business. Spirituality is becoming more and common in everyday conversations at home and at work. The concepts that spirituality offers transcend the various divisions that exist among formalized religions. More and more people are looking to find the universal spirituality that seems to resonate deep within all of us. We are finding that true spirituality can not only be found in church, but in all aspects of life.

Personally, I have noticed that more and more people are open to and curious about a spirituality that isn't driven by rules, regulations, dogma, and ritual. People are interested in living an honorable life, striving for improvement, and knowing that if the world is going to improve, they themselves need to improve.

One of the questions that I feel all CEOs, and everyone for that matter, might consider is what legacy will they leave behind when they finish their career and life. How will the world remember them and the way they lived their lives? While I don't think it is important that we make our life's decisions based on what other people think, it is noble to be mindful of living a life that we feel is healthy and contributes to the improvement of the world. Some questions for all of us to consider:

When we die, how do we want the world to remember us?

Personally?

Professionally?

How would we want to be remembered in the way that we did business?

As a CEO and emerging Corporate Samurai, what type of legacy would we like to leave in this world?

I have found one of the most wonderful exercises along these lines is to sit down with a piece of paper and close your eyes. Spend a couple of minutes getting quiet and slowing the mind down. Once quiet, allow your pen to move across the paper effortlessly as you take dictation of the words that come to your head as you write *your obituary.* Write the obituary you would like to see at the time you would choose to step off this world.

When I project myself into the future and I imagine myself in my last days, I don't think I will be concerned with how much money I made or how many houses I accumulated. I strongly feel that what I will be concerned with will be the quality with which I lived my life. I will be thinking about the people I was involved with and how I treated them. I strongly believe I will look back on what my *mindful intent* was when I was doing the things I was doing.

I want to know that I constantly looked at ways to come to know myself deeper and that I took the time to discover the delicate intricacies of what it means to be human.

I want to remember the honest flow of emotion as life swept over me with all its glory. I want to know that I lived a rich, full life filled with experiences that helped me appreciate who I am and the people closest to me. I want to remember the quality moments I had with family and friends and co-workers. I want to relive again those wonderful moments I had when I was able to say or do something that made someone's life just a little bit easier. I want to relish those moments when I was

I want to know in my heart that I took the time to give deeply of myself in the process that is this game called life, that I was not afraid to risk the image of who I thought I was at the time to get a better sense of my life's mission.

present at a major life event, totally present and grateful to be there with others—whether it was a marriage, funeral, rite of passage, or just being right there in body and spirit when someone truly needed me.

I want to remember my life and my businesses as purposeful and driven to provide help, support, and opportunities. I want my professional career to follow my personal life in that, in both, I continually strived to give from the best and deepest parts of my being. I want to know that I worked with joy in my heart and never took for granted the incredible gifts that came to me by just being human. I want to know beyond a shadow of a doubt that I lived a life of honor, integrity, love, and compassion and that I looked to improve the world through my vision.

We in America don't realize how fortunate we are to have the freedoms and opportunities that we do. We've lost a sense of perspective.

Someone once told me that one out of twenty people born in the world are born here in the United States. Imagine you were waiting to be born into your body. You're standing in front of a long table, and the guardian who lets you into the world says something like this:

"If you want to be born in the United States, I'm going to hand you this twenty-sided die. You tell me what number is going to come up, and if you're lucky, you'll guess right and be born in the United States."

If we use that metaphor, each one of us privileged enough to be born here stepped up, called out our number, promptly rolled that twenty-sided die and, sure enough, our number came up.

Sometimes I forget how fortunate I am to be living the life that I've lived.

By no means am I financially rich at this point in my life.

However, I am *rich*.

I am rich with a loving wife who has stood by me for twenty-eight years through the good times and the bad—and we have truly had our share of difficult and painful times.

I am rich with two beautiful children with whom I am deeply in love, and am so honored to be their father.

I am rich in the fact that, at forty-seven years old, I can still do virtually anything I could do at twenty. Granted, I can't run as fast or jump as high, but I can shoot a basketball better than I did when I played in high school. I am a better all-around martial artist than I was when I was twenty.
I am rich in that my mind still works and my overall health is excellent.

I am rich in that I have family and friends who love me and support me in pursuit of my dreams.

I am rich in my awareness that the Divine Intelligence that makes up the fabric of all reality is close to me every moment as I walk through life.

I am rich in my gratitude for the acceptance I have for all people and all life, knowing that we are all one.

And lastly, *I am rich* knowing that my path in life is to strive to do the best I can, to honor everyone who comes in contact with me, and to do whatever I can to make this world a better place for everyone.

I'll tell you a secret that I personally don't think is much of a secret: the things that I mentioned above about being rich with are 99% of what *each and every one of us could also say*. Well, some of us may not be in better physical shape now than we were at twenty, but in most ways mentioned above, you too can have the same richness in your own life.

I won't speculate on the number, but my guess is that very few CEOs truly feel they are rich in all the ways mentioned above. Most have worked and sacrificed and may strongly feel that in some ways, they are deeply out of balance. Their personal life may be suffering, or their sense of service may be out of whack. They may communicate like a politician and give nobody a straight answer. They've learned to play the corporate game, and, unfortunately for a lot of CEOs, it's a nasty game that takes a terrible toll on their life, and the life of their families.

Our legacy as Corporate Samurai is to leave behind a business that honors each component of our organization. It is also our legacy to leave behind family, friends, and a community that will remember us for what we did and how we did it and not just how much money we made. We leave behind a mission to continue the Corporate Samurai philosophy, which is rooted in compassion, honesty, integrity, love, and a vision that is inclusive and expansive and serves the greater good of all.

We walk the path unafraid of the obstacles of life. We fight with every ounce of our being to come from the highest consciousness we can imagine as we look to follow the great modern Samurai that came before us. Human beings who may not have considered the term "Samurai" have the ability to step up and walk the path of compassion, honesty, integrity, love, and a vision to make the world a better place—a Samurai for the new millennium.

We can aspire to be like Dr. Martin Luther King, Mother Teresa, Mahatma Gandhi, and countless others who lived life from the wisdom and love in their hearts, like those who stood up to make the world a better place for all, not just a select few or those with money—all of us.

I humbly stand before you and ask that you look deep in your heart and see the person you always wanted to be. See the person your parents wanted you to be, and step into the role and begin living it.

It's time to rediscover the depth of our being and to honor the potential inside of us. It's time to step up and become the Corporate Samurai we were destined to be.

Remember: inside us is the greatest human being we have ever imagined.

Conclusion

We are all Corporate Samurai, no matter if we are running corporations or working in them, as we are the Divine walking this path. Inside us is the greatest human being we have ever imagined. Sometimes we forget this and allow decisions to influence the wonderful model inside of us and allow dishonorable qualities to move into our thoughts, words, and actions. Misdirection, confusion, lack of honoring of our emotions, poor communication, greed, pride, inauthentic interactions, ego, and self-centeredness can slowly invade our consciousness.

We must be diligent in our mindfulness of the path we desire to walk and mindfulness in making moment-to-moment choices that resonate with our deepest wishes in living our life.

I am honored to be evolving on my own path of a Corporate Samurai. I will continue to strive to reach out to the world with an open heart, open arms, and an open mind. I will continue to train in the ways of the Samurai as I move through my life inside and outside the business world and honor those who choose to walk this path with me.

I ask you to look closely at the life and the work environment you've chosen. What can you do to bring an evolving sense of consciousness to your life and your organization?" Are you willing to begin the walk the Samurai path may offer? If so, I applaud you from the deepest part of my heart. I know it is not easy to walk the way of the Corporate Samurai.

*Are you willing to begin the walk
the Samurai path may offer?*

However, sometimes the victory is not measured in the outcome but in the adventure that is presented along the way. The path of Corporate Samurai is not for the weak of heart or those with a weak constitution. It is for those individuals who want everything out of life and are willing to look into the depths of their being to discover the perfection within. It is for those who are willing to find beauty in every step, every word, and every document and then wish to share this gift. It is for those of us who truly wish to make the world a better place and are willing to start within our own organization.

I hope this is you!

I look forward to seeing you in the corporate world, at a seminar, fundraiser, community event, or any place we may meet. I look forward to bowing in admiration, compassion, and respect as I learn of your ascension to the ranks of the Corporate Samurai. Until then, may the universe continually give you what you want in the deepest fiber of your being.

About the Author

Ray Faulkenberry was born and raised in the San Francisco Bay Area and continues to live there today with his wife, Linda, son, Wesley, and daughter, Meaghan. He graduated from Clayton Valley High School before heading off to Los Medanos Community College, California State University at Sacramento, and then the Rosebridge School of Integrative Psychology (now Argosy University). Ray earned a PhD in psychology, where he specialized in psychological/spiritual counseling and communication theory, particularly in relation to organizational development.

He has taught martial arts for over twenty years and achieved his seventh-degree black belt in Tae Kwon Do and Kenpo. He has also received black belts in Tai Chi and traditional ancient weapons. In June of 2005, Ray became an ordained Interfaith Minister and looks to bring universal spiritual principles into the work environment and everyday life. He is a deep believer in the quantum model of the universe and believes the concepts of intention and inspiration are vital in evolving both oneself and one's business.

He has worked with various populations as a consultant, teacher, trainer, counselor, and mediator. He is the founder of several organizations designed to bring about transformation and change in a positive way:

Conscious Media, Inc.—A corporation designed to share media that stimulates, engages, educates, and entertains, through various media channels that will include but not be limited to books, seminars, radio, film, television, newspapers, magazines, and the Internet.

We R One Productions—A multimedia production company designed to produce commercially viable, exciting, inspirational films.

The Institute for World Transformation—A nonprofit organization designed to provide services and research to support organizations desiring transformation.

Steps of Life—A youth-development organization designed to provide various opportunities for at-risk populations.

Innerspec—A prototypical software company specializing in psychological and educational assessment tools.

Aside from developing his businesses, Ray consults, speaks and provides training for people and companies passionate about life, communication, productivity, empowerment, education, leadership, team-building, and spirituality. He can be contacted through his web site, www.rayfaulkenberry.com.

BIBLIOGRAPHY

Covey, Stephen. *The Seven Habits of Highly Successful People*, 1st Edition. New York, NY: Simon and Schuster, 1989.

Friedman, Cyrus. *The Trillion Dollar Enterprise: How the Alliance Revolution Will Transform Global Business.* New York, NY: Perseus Books HarperCollins, 1998.

Mitroff, Ira and Elizabeth Denton. *A Spiritual Audit of Corporate America: A Hard Look at Spirituality, Religion, and Values in the Workplace.* San Francisco, CA: Josey-Bass Inc., 1999.

IRVINE, Calif., Jan. 18 /PRNewswire/—Only 6% of Americans say they love their jobs. Anywhere from 50 to 90% say they are job haters, depending on the survey. According to a Gallup Poll, with similar findings reported by *Entrepreneur Magazine*, approximately 77% of Americans hate their jobs. This reality costs American companies over $300 billion annually in stress related claims. And this doesn't even consider the costs in terms of absenteeism, turnover, and the loss of creativity and productivity.

Entrepreneur Magazine, January 18, 2007 "Why 77% Of Americans Hate Are Job Haters ... 4 Steps To Making Work Work" By Scott Hunter. Only 6% of Americans say they love their jobs. Anywhere from 50 to 90% say they are job haters, depending on the survey. According to a Gallup Poll, as reported by *Entrepreneur Magazine*, approximately 77% of Americans hate their job.

The definition of business
University of Georgetown Business
http://uis.georgetown.edu/departments/eets/dw/GLOS-SARY0816.html

Warren Buffett, the world's second richest man is giving away most of his fortune to the Bill and Melinda Gates Foundation. http://money.cnn.com/2006/06/25/magazines/fortune/char-ity1.fortune/

Business Wire. "Majority of Adults Believe Spirituality at Work is Beneficial; Survey shows most adults have a daily spiritual practice and say spirituality would help workplaces." http://findarticles.com/p/articles/mi_m0EIN/is_2003_March_14/ai_98757882, March 14, 2003.

FOOTNOTES

[1] The definition of business
University of Georgetown Business
http://uis.georgetown.edu/departments/eets/dw/GLOS-SARY0816.html

[2] Warren Buffett, the world's second richest man is giving away most of his fortune to the Bill and Melinda Gates Foundation. http://money.cnn.com/2006/06/25/magazines/fortune/charity1.fortune/

[3] Definition of Integrity: this definition can be found at: http://www.brainyquote.com/words/in/integrity179449.html.

[4] Covey Stephen, *The Seven Habits of Highly Successful People*, (New York, NY Simon and Schuster, 1989).

[5] Mitroff, Ira and Elizabeth Denton. *A Spiritual Audit of Corporate America: A Hard Look at Spirituality, Religion, and Values in the Workplace.* (San Francisco, CA: Josey-Bass Inc., 1999)

[6] Business Wire. "Majority of Adults Believe Spirituality at Work is Beneficial; Survey shows most adults have a daily spiritual practice and say spirituality would help workplaces."http://findarticles.com/p/articles/mi_m0EIN/is_2003_March_14/ai_98757882, March 14, 2003.

[7] Friedman, Cyrus. *The Trillion Dollar Enterprise: How the Alliance Revolution Will Transform Global Business.* (New York, NY: Perseus Books HarperCollins, 1998.)

CONGRATULATIONS!
Take advantage of these amazing gifts!

I'd like to help you get started NOW so I'm offering you 2 FREE, no obligation gifts. The first one is a FREE 30 minute ONE ON ONE strategy session in which I or one of my trained coaches will personally work with you.

During this amazing session you will:

- Uncover your hidden talents that will catapult you farther done the Corporate Samurai Path
- Learn how what you are currently doing is holding you and your company back
- Decide on an appropriate action plan to move you and your company towards its highest potential.

Let's get started now!
Just call me at 925-457-8213 or send me an email to
CorporateSamurai@comcast.net

YOUR SECOND GIFT!
Go to rayfaulkenberry.com under CONQUER and register and receive a free mp3 file which provides a wonderful 60 minutes of information about how you can personally develop using the Corporate Samurai process. Once there, you can also log into the Samurai philosophies, videos, messages, and other tools to help you and your business succeed!

CONGRATULATIONS! YOU AND YOUR
COMPANY ARE ON YOUR WAY!

Corporate Samurai Coaching

Wouldn't it be great to have a trusted guide and mentor who could help walk you through the steps to becoming a true *Corporate Samurai?* To be able to have someone to hold your hand and guide you through the difficult spots in achieving the necessary results that you're looking for?

Becoming a *Corporate Samurai* is the greatest thing you can do for yourself, your company, and your family.

Growing into a *Corporate Samurai* is like taking a trip, if you do your research before setting out you'll be mindful of the potential detours, roadblocks, and possible traffic jams; while taking a trip without proper planning can leave you disabled on the side of the road. Of course, even the best planned routes can lead down unexpected paths.

Corporate Samurai Coaching WILL SHOW YOU:

- The Steps needed to become a Corporate Samurai

- How to communicate better in all areas of your life

- The nuts and bolts of empowering others

- How to create a company your employees and consumers will love

- Ways of creating a legacy that lives far beyond you

- How to find joy in every phase of your life while your "Bottom Line" soars!

In our *Corporate Samurai Coaching Program* you will work with me (I have a handful of openings a year) or one of my highly trained personal Samurai coaches who will help guide you and your company down the road to success.

If you're finally ready to get off the fence and create a new you that will affect every facet of your life from your personal relationships to your business dreams then the *Corporate Samurai Coaching Program* is EXACTLY what you need."

CALL 925-457-8213 TODAY FOR YOUR FREE STRATEGY SESSION TODAY!

www.ingramcontent.com/pod-product-compliance
Lightning Source LLC
Chambersburg PA
CBHW020812300326
41914CB00075B/1698/J